The
MUSIC
MANN

MY LIFE IN SONG

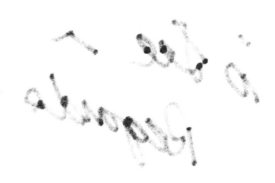

Printed in the United States of America
First Edition, First Printing, June 2013
ISBN: 978-1-4675-7420-4

John and Betty Mann
117 James Lawrence Orr Drive
Anderson, SC 29621-1809
www.johnnymannsingers.com

Cover illustration: Buzz Gambill
Cover design: Caryn Scheving
Printed by PIP Printing and Marketing, Anderson, SC

The

MUSIC
MANN

MY LIFE IN SONG

Johnny Mann
as told to Kathryn Smith

To Lil and Betty

They made me do it –
practice piano and write this book!

CONTENTS

INTRODUCTION

America was abuzz on June 18, 1973, and much attention was on the White House. That morning, President Richard M. Nixon welcomed General Secretary Leonid I. Brezhnev for the first official state visit by the head of the U.S.S.R. to America since Nikita Krushchev in 1959. It would be a long summer for Nixon, as the Watergate hearings commenced later that month, but he was focused that day on the historic meeting with Brezhnev.

Brezhnev's White House visit was part of an extended tour that included stops at Camp David and the Western White House at San Clemente, California. In between star-studded social events and sight-seeing, the leaders had serious talks about issues such as nuclear weapons.

Though neither of them knew it at the time, Nixon would leave office in disgrace a little over a year in the future.

Wait a minute, you're probably wondering. Isn't this supposed to be a book about music? What's up with the history lesson?

Well, music plays a big part in our country's history, and this was one of those times. At the official state dinner on June 18th, Secretary Brezhnev, President and Mrs. Nixon and their many guests were entertained by a choral group I led called the Johnny Mann Singers. Following the dinner of beef Bordelaise and various side dishes – the menu was written half in French and half in English for some reason – my eighteen wholesome, talented singers performed medleys of popular, Broadway and patriotic music. We ended with "The Battle Hymn of the Republic," which might have reminded Secretary Brezhnev just what kind of a country he was dealing with.

But he wasn't paying attention to the words of the music. In fact, he didn't speak or understand much English. He was ogling the girls in my group in their red and white costumes and knee-high go-go boots.

After the performance, Brezhnev and Nixon came up on stage to meet the performers. The Soviet leader was chuckling and President Nixon asked his interpreter what he was laughing about. The interpreter said, "He likes the girls in the short skirts."

A number of important agreements were signed during the visit, which marked a major thaw in the Cold War that had begun after World War II. Perhaps Brezhnev's warm response to my group had something to do with it. At any rate, it was one of the highlights of my life, and I never would have imagined that music would bring me to such a place when I was a young kid balking at my mother's insistence that I practice the piano. What a country we have!

As an admitted procrastinator about everything other than music, it has taken me a lot of years to even think about writing a book. The many requests I've had from people to share my stories were just treated with polite humility. Then, along came Dr. David Van Gorder, Psy.D, who sat me down at his home with a tape recorder and made me "Talk!" and answer a multitude of questions about my birth, background and career. This was in the 1990s.

Those cassette tapes sat in my desk glaring at me with an occasional "gentle prompting" from my wife Betty to get started on the book. After all, I did have plenty of time on my hands, and I might die before I could get all these remembrances into the hands of my family and friends. Now, senior moments and memory lapses don't help when trying to recall events from so many years ago, but as I faced my eighty-fifth birthday this year, I sat down with Betty, our friend Kathryn Smith and a tape recorder (except they don't use tape anymore!) and talked again. We've finally gotten this book into print.

This is an honest accounting of my long and eventful life. Because of my love of people and tendency to trust them, I've made mistakes and errors in my life that I'm not proud of. I've never had a mentor, counselor or advisor I could turn to either personally or professionally, and I readily admit to being too gullible at times. As a result, I have had to suffer (and still do!) the consequences of some of my self-injuring decisions. But even at the worst of times, I've been guided and cared for by God. I'm just like the saying on the U.S. currency – In God I Trust! My love of God, my country and my music are the underpinnings of my life. For the past thirty years, I've been blessed to have my wonderful Betty at my side, and that has made a huge difference. She is the love of my life.

As you read, it is my hope that you will see how fortunate I have been to travel many avenues of music that included singing, writing, arranging, composing, conducting, producing radio jingles, making product commercials, doing voiceovers and appearing in television series while getting to know some of the most interesting, entertaining and famous people one could ever hope to meet. I have been blessed many times over and feel so grateful for the opportunities I have had and the musical talent God gave me.

Thanks for your interest in my life story!

John Mann
June 2013
Anderson, South Carolina

Chapter One

BORN INTO MUSIC

My musical talent is a gift from God, but also a gift from my mother and father, Lillian and Ellsworth Franklin Mann. Lil and Ells were both enormously talented musically. Love of music began for my mother when she was a little girl and her father made her sit at the piano.

He would open a hymnal and tell her to play it by sight-reading. He pushed her into that, but she did go to the Peabody Conservatory in Baltimore where she studied voice, piano and organ. Lil worked all her life in music as a teacher, performer, choir director and musical director of Gilbert and Sullivan operettas.

She did the same thing to me when I was a boy that her father had done to her, making me stay at the piano

My parents, Ellsworth Franklin Mann and Lillian Howard Mann

when I wanted to go outside and play football. I'd say, "Aw, Mom," and she would say, "Sit down! Practice!"

Ells, as I said, was also very talented. He sang bass in a church choir and he could play the piano by ear. Not just the melody, he'd play the chords that created the harmony, too. But he could only read music in a very limited way. Ells was a carpenter and did odd jobs. He just surfed along and barely made ends meet. Lil was his second wife; I don't know anything about his first wife. My father brought my half-brother, Ellsworth Franklin Mann, Jr., to Lil to raise when he was a year old. He was known

A great brother, Nick

as Nick because he said, "No one is going to call me Ellsworth!" He was nine when I was born so we were raised together. I loved him so much!

My parents both sang in the choir at Emmanuel Episcopal Church in Baltimore, the choir that sang over me when I was baptized in 1928. We lived in a row house at 2924 Ellicott Drive, with parents, Nick, my maternal grandmother and grandfather and my aunt and uncle all at the same address. There was only one toilet, and all of the adults were smokers.

I tried a cigarette once with the boy next door, Bill Armentrout. His mother had taught him to blow smoke rings to entertain the ladies at her bridge club. He was doing that when he was six and he offered to teach me. So he took a pack of cigarettes and we ran out the back door across the alley and up behind the garages. He lit the cigarette and went puff puff puff and said, "OK, that's what you do. Now you try it."

When I tried, the smoke didn't even get past my tongue because it shut off my windpipe. I said, "Wow! This is crazy. I'm not doing this." Which is a good thing because it would have ruined my voice and I'd probably have died a long time ago.

I began singing in the church choir at St. Michael and All Angels

Choir boy at Old St. Paul's Episcopal
Church in Baltimore, Maryland

Episcopal Church when I was five. So my experience in choral singing began very early and it continued non-stop until I got out of the army in 1953. I went to public school for a couple of years, and then Lil got an audition for me with the choir director of Old St. Paul's Episcopal Church, which had a school. That got me a scholarship to the school when I was eight. It was a private boys' school with only 205 boys in fourth grade through high school. With my choir scholarship the cost was $250 instead of $500 a year. But my father had left my mother by then so it was a real struggle for her.

Ells married a third wife and later on he married a fourth, Dorie. They had a daughter named Josephine. I loved Dorie – she was so much fun. My dad was just a marrying man. He was a very sweet, nice man but he was a bit promiscuous. My mother never married again. She told me, "He had a way of making me feel loved, like I was the only woman in the world." They stayed friends, but he wasn't much help with child support after he left. Some days when I was taking the streetcar to public school, I'd see my dad driving alongside in his 1936 Ford. I'd wave at him and I'd get off at the next stop and ride to school with him the rest of the way. And it was a big treat for me because I loved him very much. Once in a while he'd have some bucks and he'd give me a five-dollar bill and say, "Give this to your mother."

After I was accepted at St. Paul's School and choir, I became a boarder at the school. Discipline and honesty were emphasized. If I broke the rules, I could expect to receive demerits, which could prevent me from going home on the weekend. At the end of each week, the demerits accumulated by each boy were posted on the bulletin board for all to see. One week when I knew I had accumulated twenty demerits, I went to Master Lewis Clarke and said, "Mr. Clarke, I had twenty 'Ds' this week but they weren't posted on the board." He looked at me and replied, "Mann, I have to give you credit for your honesty in telling me this. I'm clearing you of them." Honesty sure paid off that day. I can't remember what I could have done to get that many demerits in one week. We had to walk thirty minutes per "D" around the track on Saturday mornings, supervised by a teacher. I would have been one tired little boy.

One way I know I earned demerits was by running all over the newly seeded football field. I didn't know I was doing anything wrong, but Mr. Howdy Meyers, the sports coach, hollered at me from his window, "Mann, that'll be three Ds!" He happened to be my next-door neighbor, so that sure didn't help at home.

At the dining table for all meals, we had to clean our plates, no matter what we were served. One evening I had a sick headache and knew I couldn't eat the Brussels sprouts that were served. I told Mr. Rhett, the supervising master, but he insisted I finish my plate. I promptly threw up. I guess he believed me then, because I wasn't reprimanded.

St. Paul's emphasis on honesty led me to confess something I did to my mother. I still have the letter I wrote to her, in pencil on lined paper. On the outside I wrote, "To Mom only – PERSONAL – Gramps or no one else can open it."

> *Dear Mom,*
> *You always said, get your school books from St. Paul's. Well the reason I didn't was at the end of last year I turned them over to the Book Store out there and got about $2.00 for them. Instead of bringing that money home I spent it. The way I spent was this: I paid off some small debts I owed and spent the rest foolishly. When I come home I am ready for any punishment I am to receive. But I will slowly but surely pay back that two dollars. I'm sorry.*
> *Johnny*

On the positive side, every year one boy was awarded the St. Paul's Choir Medal of Honor with his name engraved on it. I was so surprised to receive that award and I still cherish it.

Those days at St. Paul's shaped me for the future, teaching me discipline and good conduct that served me well in the National Guard and the army. I'm sorry kids today aren't raised with this sort of discipline.

I went back to public school in seventh grade and I finished my education at Baltimore City College in 1947. That was the name of it, but it was a high school. That's where I got my first exposure to pop music, the piano blues called boogie-woogie. I'd been practicing the piano since I was six or seven with Lil, but I didn't enjoy it because I wanted to be out in the dirt playing football with my friends. But she would say, "Sit down," just as her father had, and I did what I was told. Now, of course, I thank God for my mom, who made my life what it is today. She and the Lord – or I should say the Lord and she – made my music world and my career in music successful because of her diligence and discipline and the talent He gave me.

Mom and an opera star from The Met named Rosa Ponselle were the co-producers of the Baltimore Civic Opera Company, and involved me in many of the Gilbert and Sullivan operettas done there. When I was in these productions with her, she'd say, "Don't call me 'Mom,'" because everyone in the production called her Lil.

I'm sure "Lil" wanted me to be a concert pianist so when I was fourteen she arranged for me to take lessons from a friend who she knew from her Peabody days. Sol Sax was the pianist for the National Symphony Orchestra in Washington, D.C. I would get up at 4 a.m. on Saturdays and take the train to Washington for a one-hour lesson and come all the way back home. Sax taught me all the technique stuff – the real hard stuff. I had to learn scales in every key with proper fingering. But I only practiced at home when my mom grabbed me by the scruff of the neck and made me practice, unless it was something I really wanted to learn.

When you are learning a new work, you have to play every bit of it over a hundred times and that's what I didn't want to do. But I learned technique from Sax so I could play the piano well. Fortunately, I always had that talent to hear a melody and just know the chords. But I can't take credit for that. God gave me that.

Sax taught me some stuff like Gershwin's "Rhapsody in Blue," but when the boogie-woogie got popular I bought some sheet music and learned to play it. Boogie-woogie was the first thing I played when the kids all said, "Gee, whiz, that's great!" And I thought, Holy mackerel, maybe that's worth considering! Then when I was fifteen a family down the street bought me a Tommy Dorsey record for my birthday. Big band music – Tommy Dorsey, Glenn Miller, Artie Shaw – was very popular in the 1940s. When I heard Tommy Dorsey's theme song, "Getting Sentimental Over You," I said to Lil, "What's that instrument?" and she said, "That's a trombone." I wanted to play like Tommy Dorsey and decided I had to have a trombone.

Lil was glad for me to be interested in some other kind of music so she rented me a trombone for three dollars a month from Ted's Music Store. The next day I went to school and I was automatically in the swing band, the marching band, the symphony and every other kind of musical combo that required a trombone. And I couldn't even hold the instrument, much less play it! But I took some lessons and practiced and as soon as I could, I started playing trombone in local orchestras around Baltimore.

One of the high school guys I knew, Gus Cocoros, was a Greek guy and a wonderful friend. He was one of the best drummers in town. We hung out a lot and we started playing in a dance band led by Bill Slade, an orchestra leader. He had three trumpets, four trombones, five saxophones and rhythm. We'd play four hours and get paid five dollars for it. We thought, man, we'd died and gone to heaven!

Then a wonderful thing happened. When I was first playing with the band I looked at that music and it was all beautifully copied on a machine. I said to one of the guys, "Where do these music charts come from?" and he said, "Arrangers do them." That was the first time I ever heard of orchestration, and immediately a light went on in my head and I said, "That's something I want to do!" Also, that's when I found out all instruments are not in the same key. You've got to know that or you

My first performing vocal group, The Overtones. Clockwise from top, Johnny Mann, Al Friday, Pudsy Schaeffer, Bill Bronson

can't write for them.

Around Christmas time, I got a job in the men's department at Stewart and Company that paid twenty-one dollars a week. Coincidentally, they had a company choir at Christmas and I joined that. After the holidays my sales job ended and Stewart's offered me a chance to stay on and learn retail management, but I said no. I wanted to pursue my music. That was the last time in my life I had a job that wasn't primarily about music – and even the sales job had a choir attached to it.

I still lived with my mom. Lil kept me from starving to death!

Around 1949, I started my own vocal group, three guys and a girl singing. These groups, like the Pied Pipers and Tommy Dorsey and the Modernaires, had gotten really popular. The Blue Mirror was a really nice downtown club in Baltimore with an oval-shaped bar and a stage in the middle of the room and that's where my group the Overtones first sang. That was the first music I began writing. Because I'd been in choirs for so many years I knew about voices, so I could write the chords. I sang one of the parts and did the arrangements. At the time I also had a job working at WAAM-TV in Baltimore as a camera man. But because of the success of the Overtones, they put us on the air singing various popular tunes.

We got some instrumental accompaniment going with Jimmy Smith on the piano and Al Friday on tenor sax and me on the trombone. Our singer was a real glamour-puss and she also had a brush on a conga drum to keep time. But it didn't work. We needed some rhythm. I had joined the National Guard right after high school and could borrow a bass from its band. The strings are G, D, A and E and I could hear all the bass notes in my head, so I could sing the harmony part and play. I'd never touched a bass in my life, and when I got going I bloodied up my fingers something awful. I had Band-Aids up to my elbows!

After that, the Overtones changed to a quartet without instruments and a different girl, Pudsy Schaeffer, Al Friday, Bill Bronson and me. We entered a talent contest in Baltimore at the Club Charles and we turned out to be the only vocal group, so we won! The prize was going to Philadelphia for two weeks to work as the introductory group to Mickey Shaughnessy. He was a very well-known night club stand-up comic. Big, wonderful, Irish guy. The gig was at Palumbo's Steakhouse, where the Philly cheese steak was first made by a guy who owned that restaurant. (Years later he became my neighbor in California.)

We got a local agent in Philadelphia after our gig with Shaughnessy ended and we got a job at Charlie Ventura's Open House with the same road crew. One night when we were playing there I ate the tuna surprise for dinner. Some surprise. I was so sick! I got up on stage to sing and I made it through the song and ran right off the stage to upchuck. That went on all through our evening gig.

While I was on the road, I missed the regular drills for the National Guard and so I was automatically inducted into the army in 1951. I had to drop what I was doing and get rid of all my stuff and go to Camp Breckenridge, Kentucky for basic training as a member of the 101st Airborne Division. And that led to another chapter of my life in music.

Chapter Two

I'M IN THE ARMY NOW

The normal army basic training lasted fourteen weeks. Now, some of the things I was doing in basic I had already done in the National Guard, but in army basic they really kick you around a lot and give you a lot of orders and you get dirty. They teach you discipline. You've seen it in the movies, the sergeant talks down to the rest of the troops like they're dogs.

One of the training exercises we did at Camp Breckenridge was tank protection. We marched out to this open field where there was a tank track and lined up beside it. In the tank track there were oil barrels stuck down in holes about every six feet or so. The sergeant told us to jump down in the holes and squat down to the bottom or else we'd get killed when the tank drove over the holes. I was in the second row of guys, and the sergeant blew his whistle and we jumped in. The problem was that after so many drills, the bottom of the hole had started to fill up with dirt and when I got in there, I couldn't squat because my legs were too long and I could only bend over a little. I called out to the sergeant, but he just yelled, "Shut the hell up!" So I just dug my heels in and got down as low as I could. As a tank moves it rolls up and down and I was really lucky that it was going up as it went over me because

US Army Field Band buddies in 1951-1953.
We're on tour looking for the Loch Ness
Monster in Loch Lomand, Scotland.

it just scratched the top of my helmet. It was a close call.

One of the first things you need to learn in the army is never to volunteer. During basic training when you were sitting around in the barracks a superior might come in, see you doing nothing and grab you up and ask you why you're just sitting around. They'd have you do something just to keep you occupied. So I took a bucket and mop and kept them in the corner. No one paid much attention to it. We were in there one afternoon and the sergeant came bursting in the door hollering. I grabbed my mop and bucket and while he was yelling at everyone else, I went right by him with my mop and bucket and he just told me to get out of the way.

Other times, I avoided assignments by just keeping my mouth shut. It was five o'clock one morning, still dark out, and raining. We were all standing at attention. The sergeant asked if anyone played the piano. Of course I did, but I knew better than to say so. But a couple of guys raised their hands. It turned out he didn't really need piano players. They had to go over to the officer's club with a rolling cart and move a piano. In the rain!

Although basic training was supposed to last fourteen weeks, mine got cut to eight in an unusual way. I was interviewed for Officer Candidate School or OCS, which is something every enlisted man was offered.

The lieutenant interviewing me asked, "Do you think you might want to become an officer sometime?" And I said, "Well, I don't think so because I think I am going to be transferred."

"Transferred?" he asked. "From basic training?" "Yes, sir," I said. "I think I might be transferred to play in the Army Field Band at Fort Meade, Maryland."

"Oh," he said. "Who is the commanding officer of that band?" I replied, "Captain Chester Whiting."

What had happened is my good friend Frank Granofsky had been in the band for many years and was going to be a career, thirty-year bandsman. I knew him from the Maryland National Guard Band. Frank was a wonderful musician. He played the violin as a kid and had absolute pitch as a singer, and he took to tympani, too. He put my name in with Captain Whiting and he requested me.

"Captain Whiting?" the lieutenant said. "Well, if he's trying to get you transferred, he might have a hard time. I don't think General Whatshisname is going to allow you to be transferred because you're in the army now and the general wants all of you men in Korea."

So I said to myself, Oh, man, that's a bummer. But what I didn't know is that the U.S. Army Field Band is a congressional unit, started during World War II when Captain Whiting was a lieutenant. They started out as maybe fifteen guys in the Pacific Islands, but by 1951 they didn't march around in the mud any more. They were strictly for big concerts and traveling. The secretary of the army in Washington was in charge of that band, and he could do whatever he wanted to do. If he wanted someone in the band, he could get them from wherever they were.

I didn't really know how any of that worked at the time, but I soon got the word to pack up, I was going to Fort Meade. And I was thrilled!

At that time, it was about an eighty-piece band and they took the men who could sing and had a thirty-voice male chorus with a choral director. I got into the band as a trombone player and I also sang. There was a staff of about three guys who wrote the orchestrations but I wasn't part of that because I was still just learning to do arranging. We sang and played all kinds of pop music from the era, choral pieces and Broadway music.

Fort Meade was right on the outskirts of Baltimore, so I lived at home with my mom and went to rehearsals. I showed up for my first rehearsal with my backpack and I got a dress uniform and staff sergeant stripes just for being in the band. A bunch of us guys would drive to rehearsals together, rehearse in the morning, go have lunch, finish up around two or three in the afternoon and that was our day.

We weren't doing much military stuff, but we did a lot of touring. We did concerts up and down the East Coast, here and there across the country, places we could go on buses. In touring we always traveled and stayed in twosomes in the hotels and they were always the finest hotels. Frank Granofsky and I were usually roomies, and it all worked out so wonderfully. It was really easy and about the best thing that ever happened to me because I could stay in Baltimore and do whatever I wanted to do. The army took precedence, of course, but I had a vocal group in my off time.

When we were on tour, if we had an evening concert we could be on our own during the day to do what we wanted, as long as we reported back as scheduled. Well, once in Florida on a hot, blistery day I was out gallivanting. I got back to the hotel and Frank said, "Hey, John, Lieutenant Bearly is looking for you. You missed the trombone meeting." I was so surprised! I didn't know there was a trombone section meeting. He told me that because I missed the meeting I wouldn't be allowed to march in the parade.

It turned out to be a real blessing. They had the parade in a big, open field and it was 110 degrees. They were all in their dress uniforms and I was in my regular clothes under a shady tree watching the band go by and smiling at them. They gave it to me when they got done. "Man," they said, "you got lucky getting thrown out of the band for one day!"

I did march in another parade, though: Dwight Eisenhower's inauguration parade in Washington in 1953. There were tons of people waiting for him to come down Pennsylvania Avenue and the Army Field Band led the way.

We also had a European tour. That was a real education for some of us.

We were riding on two large buses and we pulled up to Le Grand

Hotel near the Opera Garnier in Paris at 10 p.m. There was a bunch of hoodlums throwing rocks at our buses. They were young French guys and they had no respect for the United States. We all rose from our seats ready to do battle, but our commanding officer made us sit down until the hotel people came out and chased the hoodlums away.

Inside the hotel, we had a larger room than usual, more like a suite, so Frank and I had a third roommate, Joe Jenkins. He was a wonderful musician, one of our orchestrators, but something of a country bumpkin. He went into the bathroom and came out and said, "Hey, Frank, what is this thing?" He was talking about the bidet. Frank said, very quickly, "Joe, it's a special sink where you wash your socks and brush your teeth." I promptly fell on the floor laughing. Boy, did we have fun!

We also went to Berlin on that tour. We were in a beautiful, exquisite hotel. After each concert we would congregate in the venue lobby or on the sidewalk and wait for our buses to take us back there. One day while I was waiting, I wrote a postcard to my mom and was looking for a place to mail it. Two girls came walking very briskly up the sidewalk speaking quickly in German. As they got close to me, I asked in German, "*Wo kann ich dies auf geben*?" which means "Where can I this up give?" One of the girls said, "Around the corner in the yellow box" in perfect English and went back to talking to her friend without even stopping.

In 1953 I got out of the army and went to Philadelphia. I met a girl there named Jean, a beautiful blonde who had won Miss Philadelphia one year. We started talking about going to California. She wanted to break into show business, and I figured there were only two places I could make music for a living, New York and Los Angeles. I figured I could starve in either place, but at least I wouldn't freeze to death in California.

I had about three hundred dollars in mustering-out pay and a car, so we packed up everything, got in the car and drove to California.

Chapter Three

GO WEST, YOUNG MANN

Jean and I drove to Hollywood and rented a studio apartment with a pull-down bed and a teeny kitchen in the corner and I started looking for music jobs before my money ran out. A few weeks after arriving, we visited Las Vegas, Jean got a job in a chorus line and that was the last I saw of her. I went back to Hollywood and moved into the YMCA for a dollar a night.

There was an agent I met who heard there was going to be a television show based on the popular comic strip *Dixie Dugan*. I said I could write a song for the pilot, and she introduced me to the first people I sang with in Hollywood. We sang it and recorded it, but the show didn't make it. In fact, if you look it up on the Internet, you won't even find information about the TV pilot or the song, just the comic strip. But I still remember the song. Here are the lyrics:

All of the fellas in town are just crazy about Dixie
'Cause Dixie is a honey with a great big sunny smile.
She has the nicest way of being, a true Irish colleen,
That's why everybody loves her, including Imogene.
So hang on to your hat and I guarantee that you'll adore her,

'Cause Dixie's got that special kind of glow.
Her lovely liltin' laughter, you'll share forever after
on The Dixie Dugan Show!

Next I got a job with a guy who was a regular piano player at a bar in Pershing Square in downtown Los Angeles. It was a little joint called Suey Welsh's Sports Club, and I got to sub for this guy playing piano for two weekends. I made sixty dollars a week, which seemed like a fortune, so I kept trying to get work playing piano. I was also trying to get some vocal work. I even auditioned for Norman Luboff, who was a famous choral director around Hollywood for motion pictures. I just went in and played the piano and sang him a ballad, but I was never a real solo singer, so he didn't hire me.

I got my first gig in Las Vegas at this time in a male quartet singing with my army friend Rex Johnson. We backed up Teresa Brewer for two weeks at The Sahara and got paid a hundred and twenty-five dollars. When I wasn't working, I collected fifteen dollars a week in unemployment. And of course seven dollars of that went to the YMCA for my room.

Then I met Ben Yost. He was a New Yorker, a very personable gentleman and fun to be around. Everyone liked him. He was a very good baritone himself and had formed a quartet called the Ben Yost Singers and booked performances for them. Then he formed other Ben Yost Singers groups – a barbershop group in straw hats and striped shirts, and the Ben Yost Cavaliers, who were dressed up with swords and boots that came up to their thighs. His wife Gerry was also a singer and had a quartet of girls.

So Ben was booking all these groups throughout the East Coast. He was so well-known for all his groups that Milton Berle told a joke about him once. He said he had gone to the theater and was surprised they didn't have any Ben Yost Singers performing.

When I met Ben, he already had a pianist. As I got to know him, I learned Ben was a good businessman and a singer, but he wasn't a musician at all. He didn't know thirteen notes. So I started to write for him and a couple of his groups. I'd go in and help with the quartet, just basic choreography so the guys wouldn't just be standing there. Not for the girls – they were better at that and did their own stuff. And I taught them how to sing their parts.

Ben had a nice big house on the hill in Studio City in the San Fernando Valley. It had an outdoor garage with a cot and its own bathroom, which I rented from him for fifteen dollars a month. That was an improvement from my old digs at the YMCA – and cheaper, too. Of course, my "roommate" was Ben's car.

Once Ben got a visit from a song-writing team, Jill Jackson and Sy Miller. They were like a lot of people who were trying to get their music published or recorded, and they hoped Ben would use it with one of his groups. He wasn't interested, but the wonderful thing is the song was "Let There Be Peace on Earth," which went on to become an internationally successful song. Because I can "hear" music in my head when I read it, I was probably the first person in the world to "hear" that song!

I spent a lot of time in the San Fernando Valley at the Doll House. It was a bar, but a classy bar, and everyone who went there became friends. We had a softball team and all that kind of stuff. Now, when you've had a drink or two, you think you can play the piano better than when you are stone cold sober. At the Doll House I would do sing-a-longs and play for people just for fun.

One night there, a man came up to me and in a very strong German accent said, "Mr. Mann, good evening." He asked me if I had done any music arranging and though I hadn't done much at the time, I said, "Yes, sir."

The man's name was Paul Sawtell. He was a composer who worked on many films, and he offered me the chance to do some work that would get my foot in the door. He and his little German wife Mimi were so sweet, and they let me stay in their guest room until he paid me. So I got to move out of the garage into a real house.

Paul would sit at the piano and write the music based on the script, a chase scene or a love scene, for example. But like many composers, he was a procrastinator, and when he was coming up on a deadline, he would have to sit at the piano and work for many hours without stopping. It wasn't a grand piano, but an upright, and he would sometimes be so tired he would doze off and hit his forehead on it. So we had this brilliant idea to tape a Kotex pad to his head so that he wouldn't hurt himself when he fell asleep. It looked strange, but it worked!

He'd write small and quickly with pencil on a big score sheet and abbreviate notations, like "ww" for woodwinds. Then he'd pass it to me and I would orchestrate it for the full orchestra. I did this for seven motion pictures, beginning with *Texas Lady* in 1955. This film starred Claudette Colbert in the title role, with Barry Sullivan, and the movie posters said, "A LADY...till the fighting started...then...WHAT A WOMAN!" I wrote the song for the film title and Les Paul and Mary Ford recorded it. That really got me because they were big recording artists at the time. That was a big hit.

My first motion picture theme song, *Texas Lady*

I got to hear the music scores during the production process, but it was the thrill of a lifetime to go to the movie theatre to see *Texas Lady* and hear my music. I shared the music credit with Paul Sawtell, even though I wrote every note of the theme song, and they spelled my name "Johnnie." Here are the lyrics:

A Texan lady came to town
And thus begins my story
She drew a hand with the best in town
Which proved to be her glory

But now the game has ended
The king has had his day
A woman's cause defended
And soon you'll hear them say

She did a man's job
But there was no doubt
She was a Texas lady.

One day the sky was hazy
Folks worthy and lazy
Came a Texas lady
To town, to town.

She smiled in all her splendor
Gave her hands so tender
Maybe God had sent her
To town.

Her heart was filled with yearning
For dreams to start anew
Love with hope returned
Were the dreams she made come true.

So now the street is shady
All is calm and hazy
Since a Texas lady
Came to town
Came to town

One of the really important results of getting the *Texas Lady* job was I could get into ASCAP – the American Society of Composers, Authors and Publishers. This organization collects royalties or reuse fees for its members, so every time a song I wrote or arranged is performed, I am supposed to get performance royalties.

Another person I met through Ben Yost was Al Goodman, who was a major television music director from New York. He had worked with

Ben Yost on countless things. Ben went and recommended me to Al and that's how I got to be the choral director on *The NBC Comedy Hour* in 1956. It was a comedy/variety show that came on every Sunday night and Jonathan Winters was one of its regular performers. All we did was show up on the day of the session, eight of us, four girls and four boys. I wrote the vocal arrangements and sang. I did the show for six months, then it was canceled. That's how I met my first studio singers.

I did a lot of studio singing, on television and for records. I'd get a call from someone who needed twelve singers, and eventually I started putting together singing groups myself. That's called being a vocal con-tractor. I sang on *The Dinah Shore Show*, and *The Lawrence Welk Show*. My first job as a studio singer in Hollywood was on a Frank Sinatra album. I was one of three guys and a girl lead picked to sing background on "Hey, Jealous Lover" and on a Christmas album for "Jingle Bells": *I love those J-I-N-G-L-E bells – BONG!*

So many people have opinions of Mr. Sinatra being a tough guy and drinking a lot. People got the impression he was a hard nose. In the studio, though, he was on time, he was very friendly and respectful and nice to the professional singers and musicians and recording staff. He was wonderful and everyone loved him. He was a total, total gentleman. Many years later I got to know him better in Palm Springs, but I'm getting ahead of myself.

I did countless recording sessions, backing up singers like Johnny Mathis, Nat King Cole, Steve Allen, Walter Brennan, Tennessee Ernie Ford, Teresa Brewer and Sammy Davis, Jr. and I was really getting busy. (Johnny Mathis had been a track star, and before he sang he'd do these high kicks as a warm-up to get his breath going!) I was moving up in my living accommodations by then. I had moved into a little apartment on Arch Drive near Ben Yost's house and later on got my own house. My mom and brother Nick moved out to California to live with me there.

In music you sometimes get some huge breaks. One of the singers I got to know was Ralph Brewster, who did vocal contracting in Hollywood. He called me to do a Union Oil commercial with one other pro singer, Lee Gotch. We sang the Union Oil song –*The pride of the 76, you'll always get the finest, the very best, the finest at the sign of the 76!* We spent

To Johnny
It was a great pleasure
working with you.
Best always   Walter Brennan

My singers were back-up voices for Walter Brennan's recording session.

an hour in the studio and we made sixty thousand dollars apiece on it!
They played it in the sports world, all the baseball games, the football
games, all those different sports complexes and we got paid a reuse
fee every time it played. That was huge, wonderful!

But for every big job like that, there were a lot of times that I'd try to get work and nothing ever came of it. There was a trumpet player I got to know who was a relation to somebody close to Judy Garland. Judy was getting ready to go to Vegas and thought she might want a piano player with her, a young guy, so I got a chance and I went to Judy's house and played for her and she sang a song. I can't remember what it was. She was very nice and sweet and she and her manager said, "We'll get back to you." Well, they never did and Judy didn't go to Vegas.

Several times I got to go with Ben Yost to come on up and see one of the most famous women in Hollywood, Mae West. Ben was very friendly with Mae, who was in her sixties by then. She was famous for her double-entendres, and her stage plays and movies always raised eyebrows and often drew the attention of censors. Her famous lines included, "Is that a gun in your pocket or are you just happy to see me?" and "I generally avoid temptation unless I can't resist it."

Mae wanted some big, good-looking lusty guys to back her up as part of her Las Vegas show. She lived really grandiose in a very classy apartment and you'd knock on the door and this great, big husky body-guard would answer. She always had two or three of these big studs there. She was always very made up and she lived in a nightgown trimmed with lots of feathers. Of course, she wouldn't have anything to do with me, I was just a skinny little kid.

Another time I ran into Elizabeth Taylor. I was going into a phone booth and she was coming out. We didn't talk. Maybe I'm lucky. I'm one of the few men she didn't marry!

I got really lucky another time during a chance encounter. It resulted in the birth of the Johnny Mann Singers. I was standing on a Hollywood street corner waiting for a light to change and started talking to a guy standing with me. I must have mentioned I was in the music business because he said, "Did you hear about Liberty Records? It's a new record company," and he gave me the address. I found out Julie London was their big star. So I put together some of the singers I was working with and I wrote out an arrangement for a song and took it into Simon Waronker at Liberty Records. And they signed my choral group up right then and there. They asked the group's name and I said "The John Mann

Singers" and they said it didn't sound good. "The Johnnie Mann Singers" rolled off the tongue more beautifully, so it became the Johnnie Mann Singers and eventually I changed the spelling to "Johnny," the way I had spelled it as a boy.

Our first album, released in 1956, was called simply *Night* and it stirred up a lot of controversy because of the provocative cover. The model, a very pretty lady named Julie Redding, was semi-nude, sitting on a bear skin rug smoking a cigarette. She was shot from behind, and you could see the curvature of her breast. It was beautiful and they put the record out and we got on the news and some people were offended. So they re-did the cover. They got another beautiful young girl who sat on a rug facing the camera but she had a nightie on. It wasn't at all sexual, just pretty.

All the titles had the word "night" in them – "The Way You Look Tonight," "In the Still of the Night," "The Night We Called it a Day," "The Night Has a Thousand Eyes." The album copy introducing me did some word play with my name: "Quite a man...this Johnnie Mann!" and predicted that "the JOHNNIE MANN Singers will soon become the top vocal group in the country."

I've been asked, "What is the Johnny Mann sound?" It's hard to describe if you aren't a composer or a musician, but I'd say my sound is a

JOHNNY MANN   Exclusive Recording Artist for

LIBERTY

Records, Inc.
Hollywood, California

My publicity photo for Liberty Records

very lush, full sound with a mixture of female and male voices. I could obtain it with various sizes of choirs. Five or six people can be lush, thirty-six people can be lush, it's a question of how I write it. I like to have a choir sound with low, very warm chords throughout, and usually I obtain this by having a male singer with a very deep voice. When the piece is bright and fast, I'd write it higher, but when you have it soft and low and beautiful, I liked to have that basso profundo voice. I'll tell you about my favorite bass singer in the next chapter.

Soon I was turning out two or even three Johnny Mann Singers albums a year, but I never really made any money on them, because the cost of the recording – the singers, the orchestra, the copyists, the studio time – is counted against sales. The only time you get paid royalties is after the costs are covered by sales. So you could make and sell lots of records and never really get anything for it except publicity.

However, that led to lots of other gigs that did pay well, and I met and worked with some of the nicest, most talented people in show business. I will share some stories about a few of these special performers in the next chapter, including a trio of surprisingly talented chipmunks.

Chapter Four

THE LADY, THE TIGER AND THE THREE CHIPMUNKS

The big name in the Liberty Records line-up in 1956 was Julie London. She was a gorgeous honey blonde who had started out as an actress but became much better known as a singer. Her voice was very sultry, and her album covers often featured her in poses showing a lot of leg. In fact, she had been a pin-up girl during World War II. She released a single in 1955, "Cry Me a River," that

Julie London's album, *Cry Me a River*

became a big hit and her signature song.

I knew Julie and her pianist, Bobby Troup, whom she later married, from a place we hung out called Monty's. Once I got involved in Liberty Records, the artists and repertoire manager Si Waronker called me on a Thursday afternoon, late, and said, "John, we're finally going to do an album with Julie London, and we're going to have strings, orchestra and singers behind Julie." We had been talking about this for some time and I knew he wanted me to do the choral arrangements.

I said "Great, when does it go?" and he said, "Monday."

"How many tunes?" I asked and he said, "Twelve tunes."

I said "You mean Monday a week?" and he said, "No, this Monday."

"Si, that's only three and a half days until the first session," I said. And Si replied, "John, do you want the job or don't you?"

Well, I did want it, so I got to work and stayed up for three days and nights writing all the choral arrangements. When I tell this story, people say, "Oh, man, you must have stayed up until one in the morning!" and I say, "You don't understand. I got NO sleep time." Fortunately I didn't have to sit at the piano so there was no need to tape a Kotex pad to my head! I did have to resort to coffee and Benzedrine, though. I didn't use bennies often, but sometimes I just had to. Then on Monday I came down to the studio with the singers and we did the session. That was the easy part!

Someone once asked me, "Did you ever have writer's block?" and I said, "What's writer's block?" If you said to me, "I'm coming into the studio day after tomorrow and I need a song," I'd sit down and do it. I wouldn't call myself a workaholic, I was just very, very busy.

I'd get calls all the time saying, "We've got a session scheduled next Monday and we need six guys and five girls to back up so-and-so," and I'd call the best singers and we'd go in and record. They were pros and could sight-read, so they didn't require much rehearsal time. Because I had gotten to know so many great pro singers around Hollywood, I could choose the very best to be part of the Johnny Mann Singers.

One of these was Thurl "Pappy" Ravenscroft, who also became one of my best friends. Pappy is the singer I mentioned in the last chapter, the one with that really deep, basso profundo voice. You may think you don't know who he is, but you would recognize his voice instantly. Here's a hint:

"They're GRRRR-ate!"

Yes, for fifty-three years Thurl was the voice of Tony the Tiger for Kellogg's Frosted Flakes. When he got really old they would send a limo

and a wheelchair and take him to
the studio. At the end of his life he
was even doing commercials in
Spanish! Thurl did a lot of Disney
movie voices, too, such as *101 Dal-
matians* and *The Aristocats* and he
sang "You're a Mean One, Mr.
Grinch!" in the TV special *Dr. Seuss'
How the Grinch Stole Christmas.*

"Pappy" and Tony

Occasionally I flew to New York
with six or eight singers to record major commercials, back in the *Mad
Men* era on Madison Avenue. We'd fly in first class, go to dinner, drink,
stay at a great hotel, record at nine the next morning and catch a one
o'clock airplane and fly home. On the plane we'd sing and play cards. It
sounds hectic, but we always had so much fun!

One afternoon we checked into our hotel rooms and then we all went
to dinner. One of the girls was having a birthday and I asked the maître
d', "We have a birthday girl, can we sing 'Happy Birthday' to her?" And
the maître d' said, "OK, just keep it low." And Thurl leaned in and rum-
bled, "How lowwwww do you want it?" in his deep, deep bass voice.

When Thurl died in 2005 at age ninety-one, Kellogg's ran an ad in
Advertising Age magazine that read, "Behind every great character is
an even greater man." That was certainly true of Thurl. A great man, a
great singer and a great friend.

We also had a married couple, Peggy Clark Schwartz, who with her
three sisters singing in close harmony performed as The Sentimentalists
with the Tommy Dorsey Orchestra in the 1940s, and her husband Wil.
He was one of the top studio saxophone players in Hollywood. Wil played
all of the woodwinds – piccolo flute, alto flute, bass flute – he was always
first chair. When he was just nineteen he was the clarinet lead for Glenn
Miller. You can hear him on "In the Mood" and a lot of Glenn Miller's
other hits. He really made the Glenn Miller sound.

Willie was famous for his clever remarks and hijinks during recording
sessions. When he heard a jazz player playing a multitude of notes that
supposedly fit together but didn't really he would say, "That's close

enough for jazz." One night he pulled a prank when he was playing in the saxophone section. Saxophones have metal clappers over holes in the instrument, each fitted with a pad to make it airtight. To play it, you blow into the mouthpiece, then depress the different clappers to produce the various notes. Every once in a while the player has to change a pad, or one comes loose or something, but you can't play without all your pads in place. Anyway, Wil was sitting beside another sax player who was heading into a major solo and when he wasn't looking, Wil dropped a spare pad on the floor between their chairs. Just when the guy was about to start, Wil whispered, "Is that one of yours?" The soloist looked down and just freaked out!

Willie was a serious smoker. All of us used to say, "OK, Wil, you need to give up smoking." He'd stop for a few days or a week but he always went back. Years later, Wil was in the hospital on his death bed, hooked up to all these machines and lines. One afternoon Peggy came to see him and said, "How are you feeling, Wil?" and he gasped out "I can't begin … to tell you … how much better I feel … since I gave up smoking."

Peggy was also very funny. One day she caught me picking my nose, trying to be discreet, and she said, "Put that back!"

Joking aside, Hollywood singers and musicians were very professional, and they were always on time. When the recording session was set to begin at eight o'clock, that meant the musicians and singers were in their seats, warmed up and ready to go, because the downbeat came at eight and the pay started at eight. I remember we had a big session one night and the No. 1 French horn player wasn't there on time. Everyone was wondering where he could be. We waited around for a few minutes, because we couldn't start without him. Finally, one of the guys went out front to look for him and found him asleep in his car. He had gotten there early! Boy, he was really embarrassed.

Another line of work I got into during the late 1950s was writing radio jingles – the tunes that go with radio station identification. I got a call from a friend at 93-KHJ in Los Angeles, Don Otis, who was just desperate. "John, I need a jingle package," he said. The musicians' union was on strike and he couldn't get any professional back-up players.

"Would you consider doing this a cappella?" I asked. "What's a cappella?" he asked. I explained it meant with voices only, no orchestra accompaniment, and that's what we did. "93-KHJ Los Angeles!" This was my first jingle for a major market and established my five- or six-note melody for the station call letters, which is called the logo. A few months ago I even got an inquiry about using one of the old jingles I'd written for a New York radio station in an episode of *Mad Men*.

In 1960 I recorded a song called "The Sound of the City" that ended with a logo of call letters that is still used sixty-three years later by

KSFO in San Francisco. My jingles have been used on radio stations all over the United States and even in some foreign countries, and I'm still writing them today, including jingles for Christian radio. In all humility, I'm referred to as "the King of the Jingle."

I started JM Productions for my jingle work. Unfortunately, one of my biggest personal mistakes in business was taking in a partner for the jingles business. Rather than paying him a 15 percent share, which was customary for an agent, I said we'd just

King of the Jingle

go 50-50. I would do the creative work and he would solicit radio stations and handle the business end from our joint bank account. It turned out he wasn't trustworthy. Not only did he take money that wasn't owed him, he later independently pedaled some of my work as his own so I didn't get paid at all. That was my supreme stupidity.

Obviously, business was not my strong suit. I had lots of money streams coming in from different sources. I never had a full-time manager or agent or even a secretary during the time I was doing all these sessions. I kept up with my own schedule with a Week-at-a-Glance book and an answering service. You've got to remember this was decades before the invention of the cell phone, so everyone in Hollywood who was singing or acting or playing was dependent on their answering services.

"Lonesome" George Gobel

In most cases, I was well compensated for my work in Hollywood and I worked with so many wonderful people. Some of my fondest memories are of George Gobel. He was a comedian who had his own television show in the 1950s, appeared often in Las Vegas and was a popular guest on talk shows. In later years he was a regular on the TV game show *Hollywood Squares*.

One of George's most famous appearances was on *The Tonight Show Starring Johnny Carson* in 1969. He was the third guest to come out. First came Bob Hope, the big star. Then Dean Martin, the big star. When George came on as a guest and sat down on the couch, Johnny said, "How are you, George?" and George's line was, "Did you ever get the feeling that the world was a tuxedo and you were a pair of brown shoes?"

George had been an instructor for fighter pilots in Oklahoma during World War II. He liked to say because of him, no Japanese plane ever got past Tulsa.

I met George in 1960. He wasn't a singer singer, but when he did his touring show he'd sing a little country song and pluck a guitar and do his comedy routine around it. Everywhere he went, I'd conduct for him. He was the sweetest man in the world, and not only that, he was funny.

We were doing a show in Chicago once and he was on stage and acted like he couldn't remember someone's name. He said, "Johnny, what's the guy's name?" and I said, "I can't remember, George," and he said, "Charlie will know. Charlie, come here!" and out came this tall Swedish model, with long platinum blond hair, wearing a sequined bathing suit. She walked out and she was six-foot-one and she was magnificent. George was about five-six and he started to say, "Charlie…" and he just stood there with his face right in her breasts. He didn't touch her, he was just looking. The audience was screaming with laughter for five minutes.

That night, George, Charlie and I went out in Chicago and had some drinks in a bar. Charlie had changed out of her bathing suit, of course, but was still just gorgeous. It was George's birthday and I had given him this big stuffed dog, and we were walking down Michigan Avenue, the three of us and the dog. An old couple came walking up the street and just after they passed us, George said, "Woof!" The old couple loved it!

George was a drinker. After his performances, he'd invite people up to his suite at the hotel. All the big stars did that. I always was there, of course, since I toured with him, but the other guests would vary from city to city. In the afternoon, he'd prepare by filling up three big bottles with water. He'd put them in the bathtub and close the curtain.

Once things got going that night, George would excuse himself from the party, leave the bathroom door cracked about an inch and then he'd take these bottles and start pouring them into the toilet. I'd sit out there knowing what was going to happen and the conversation would eventually get quieter and quieter until everyone was just listening to this torrent of water that went on and on. Then he'd walk out with this little smile on his face. It just tore the place apart!

With all that was going on in my professional career, I hadn't given much thought to getting married. In the late 1950s, Mom had come out to California and moved in with me, and later on Nick joined us and we all lived together. By 1960, I was thirty-two, and all my married friends started telling me I needed to find a wife and settle down. Through Roy

Hollingsworth, my good friend from Universal Pictures, I met a very pretty starlet named Lori Nelson.

Lori had been a beauty queen in New Mexico and became a studio contract player, like Burt Reynolds and Tab Hunter at that time. She was what you'd call a B-list actress, appearing in movies like *Revenge of the Creature* and *Hot Rod Girl.* She had also appeared on a television series with Barbara Eden and Merry Anders based on the movie *How to Marry a Millionaire.*

Her parents were very nice and she was a respectable girl. We started going out and though I wasn't really in love and wasn't ready to settle down, we got married in 1960. My mom and Nick stayed in my old house and I bought some acreage and a bigger house in Chatsworth, California. Lori put her career on hold and we started having a family. Our daughter Lori Susan was born in 1962 and Jennifer Lee was born in 1965.

Something else that happened during this time was that I became the voice of a chipmunk. Ross Bagdasarian, Sr. was a novelty song writer at Liberty Records whose hits included "The Witch Doctor." In 1958 he had this crazy idea about doing a Christmas song with a singing trio of chipmunks, Alvin, Theodore and Simon. You still hear it all the time. It's called "Christmas Don't Be Late," and has the bit about "I just want a hula hoop," which was one of the most popular toys on kids' Christmas lists that year. "Christmas Don't Be Late" came out as a single in December 1958, sold 4.5 million copies, hit No. 1 on the charts and won the award for best engineering of a record at the very first Grammy Awards in 1959.

Ross did the voices of all the chipmunks on the first recording and released a few singles later on. His professional name was Dave Seville, so he was also the voice of the chipmunks' manager, Dave, who was always yelling, "Alvin!" Ross didn't look much like the cartoon version of Dave, who was tall, thin and had a head full of dark hair. He was short, round-faced and didn't have a lot of hair.

In 1962 and 1963, I worked with Ross and Alan Davies, a pro singer, and we recorded two albums of Chipmunks Christmas songs. *Christmas with the Chipmunks* included that first hit and a lot of others, like

"(All I Want for Christmas is) My Two Front Teeth," "Jingle Bells," and "Frosty the Snowman." Ross was the voice of Alvin, I was Theodore and Alan was Simon. The names of the chipmunks came from Liberty Records executives: Alvin was named for Al Bennett, the president of Liberty Records; Theodore was named for Ted Keep, the head recording engineer; and Simon was named for Si Waronker,

The first of my two Grammys

who I've mentioned earlier was head of artists and repertoire.

I also wrote a song on the second Christmas album called "Hang Up Your Stockin'." You can get these two albums on CD today, but you won't hear "Hang Up Your Stockin'" except on the original vinyl version – if you've still got something to play vinyl on. (This way they didn't have to pay me any royalties when they sell the album. Sneaky, huh?)

Many people ask how we sang the chipmunk recordings. We would record the orchestra background of the song at 15 ips – that's inches of tape per second. Then when the orchestra was perfect, we would sing the voices very slowly and precisely over a track at 7 ½ ips. Ross sang the melody and then Al and I would be on both sides of the melody doing the harmony. It was very simple writing, trio writing. At completion, the finished recordings would be brought back to 15 ips. Then the orchestra sounded normal but the chipmunks were high-pitched and squeaky.

It's funny what a big impression my small part in Alvin and the Chipmunks has on people. In my music career, I worked with some of the biggest names in the business, recorded forty albums, won two Grammy awards, performed at the White House twice and had my own television show, but people often get the most excited to know I was the voice of Theodore! (Incidentally, I won my first Grammy Award in 1961 for best performance by a chorus, *Great Band with Great Voices*. The album was nominated in two other categories. Ultimately, I would win another Grammy in 1967 and be nominated for three others.)

But I'm getting way ahead of myself. First I've got to tell you about Danny and Joey.

Chapter Five

DANNY AND JOEY

My last chapter ended on a light note, talking about the 1963 *Christmas with the Chipmunks 2* album. But of course every American who was alive then remembers November 22, 1963, the terrible day that President John F. Kennedy was assassinated in Dallas, Texas. I was living in Chatsworth, California then, and for the life of me I cannot remember exactly what I was doing. But my reaction, after I got over my shock, was to sit down and write a song. It's called "The Voice of Freedom":

The voice of freedom is heard in our land,
A voice ringing strong and clear,
The strength of our people, a word of our God,
For all the world to hear.
A gift from our fathers passed away
To speak in a freer land by far.
The wisdom in their words will ever stay
With us who now must follow their star.
The voice of freedom will speak again,
Through us all the world shall hear.

And now is the time that voice should be heard
For our home, our country and our God.

Words and music by Johnny Mann, ASCAP, 1963

The Johnny Mann Singers recorded the song and performed it many times, once at the White House. It was the first of a number of patriotic songs I wrote, for I do love my country, my God and our freedom.

Jennifer, me, and Susie

Lori, our daughter Susie and I were by then living in a house on a hill, surrounded by six and a half acres of land. The house had a rustic California look, lots of stone and glass, with a cathedral ceiling. From one side we had a great view of the whole San Fernando Valley. At night the lights were just amazing to see. The view on the other side was mountains and grass. I built a little guest house for our live-in maids, and eventually bought another twelve acres and a pond. And of course we had a pool. In 1965 our second daughter Jennifer Lee came along. We had two German shepherds, Hoss and Moose, given to me as pups, one in each hand, who took it upon themselves to be the guardians of the girls. Wherever the girls were playing, Hoss and Moose could be found standing guard.

I had some neighbors there, though none of them were very close because of all the land around our homes. They included the actors Chad Everett and Dale Robertson, the comedian Redd Foxx, legendary song and dance man Fred Astaire and Veronica Lake. Do you remember Veronica Lake? She was a very popular actress in the 1940s who wore her blond hair over one eye. So many women who worked in munitions plants during World War II imitated her that the government asked her to change her hair style. Her fans were getting their hair tangled up in the machinery and it was dangerous for them!

Another of my neighbors was the inventor of the Philly cheese steak sandwich – the same guy who owned the Philadelphia restaurant where I got that first big break back when I was a kid leading a singing quartet in Baltimore. I remember buying his sandwiches for a quarter. He'd sold a lot of them to afford his home in Chatsworth!

In 1963 I got a call to do some work for the entertainer Danny Kaye. He was a singer and dancer and just a funny guy. His movie career was fading a bit, but he was very popular on television and with live audiences. I wrote an arrangement of "Dixie" with the Johnny Mann Singers as back-up for Danny, then I went on a twelve-week tour conducting for him and worked on his television variety show, which appeared on CBS for four years beginning in the fall of 1963.

Every night after the show, Danny wanted to go to a Chinese restaurant and he'd take over the kitchen. He'd end up knowing all the big

Me with Hoss & Moose in Chatsworth, California

Chinese restaurant owners, and in his home he converted his kitchen into one worthy of a Chinese restaurant. He just loved Chinese food and he loved to cook. Once he severely burned his leg from a cooking accident and had to appear on the show with a bandage on his leg!

Danny had an entourage and even though I wasn't part of it, he often invited me to go out with them after the show. One night I said thanks, but I already had plans. Danny winked at me and said, "Oh, you want to go get your cane varnished?"

I can't imagine what he meant. I didn't even own a walking cane, and where on earth would you go to get one varnished?

He loved to play golf, and I'd taken it up by then. He also had his own plane and loved to fly, so sometimes he would combine these two interests. One day he called me up and said, "What are you doing today? You wanna hit some golf balls? I'll meet you at Van Nuys." So we met at the airport there, flew to Palm Springs, hit a bucket of balls, had lunch and came home. He loved my mother, and would spend time just talking to Lil, and he was just wonderful to me.

Danny's humor was very physical and he was a great mimic. I always like to keep my good suit pants with a nice crease, so I'd adjust the fabric over my knees just so when I sat down. That way my pants wouldn't wrinkle. After Danny knew me awhile, he'd sit down beside me and look at me and then mimic the way I adjusted my pants. He was so clever improvising like that. When he did a show in England, all he did was be introduced, walk out, sit on the edge of the stage with his feet hanging

Me with Pete Fountain and Danny Kaye

over the side and just talk. Danny was king of the world for a while, especially in the United Kingdom. The British just loved him.

The Danny Kaye Show was a variety show, but heavier on the comedy stuff than music. Harvey Korman, who later became part of Carol Burnett's variety show ensemble, was a regular supporting player, and comic actors such as Don Knotts and Tim Conway came on to appear in skits. I was in charge of the twelve-voice vocal group and the vocal arrangements. I'd write some arrangement for Danny and his musical guest star and me to perform. Pete Fountain the clarinet player was one of

Roy and Diane Hollingsworth

those guests and the singer Diahann Carroll was another I remember well. It was part-time work, though, which enabled me to keep up all the recording I was doing all over town during the daytime.

I made the acquaintance of a really interesting man about this time, once again through my friend Roy Hollingsworth and his wife Diane. His name was Jerry Henderson. He was Roy's stepfather, and he was a very successful businessman with Avon Cosmetics and other ventures. He made a lot of money with them. Perhaps because he worried about security or just the whole atmosphere of the Cold War that was developing, he got interested in living underground.

Jerry had two underground homes built, one in Colorado and one in Las Vegas. I visited both of them, and they were just gorgeous.

The people he hired to build his home in Colorado took a mountain and built a whole house underneath that you reached by elevator. The one in Vegas had a guest house as well as the main house, a swimming pool and a waterfall that went into the pool, even a barbecue grill and putting green.

When the 1964 World's Fair came around in New York, Jerry sponsored the construction of an underground house there. I wrote a song called "The Bottom of the Fair" and Liberty Records put out a special album called *The Greatest of the Johnny Mann Singers at the Bottom of the Fair* that was sold as a promotion at the exhibit. The songs on the album included "Hello, Dolly!" and "Walk Right In," which had a great part for Pappy Ravenscroft with that Tony the Tiger voice of his.

Of course, underground living never really took off in this country, though a lot of people built bomb shelters in their backyards, and Jerry eventually began living above ground again. He loved the Johnny Mann Singers, and his name will come up again later in my story, so don't forget it.

I was still working with Danny Kaye, but he wanted more of my time than I was willing to commit. I was so busy and the Johnny Mann Singers albums were doing well. We got another Grammy nomination in 1966 for *A Man and a Woman*. I didn't want to be tied down to one thing, so I quit and they hired someone else. The show was canceled in 1967. It was sort of providence, because the very next thing that came up was *The Joey Bishop Show*.

Joey Bishop was a comic and a member of the Rat Pack. The best-known members were, of course, Frank Sinatra, Dean Martin and Sammy Davis, Jr., but Joey and the actor Peter Lawford were also members. They performed shows together live and appeared in movies like *Ocean's Eleven*. Joey had a sitcom in the early 1960s that featured him playing a comedian. He was also one of the most frequent guest hosts on *The Tonight Show Starring Johnny Carson* on NBC. Then ABC decided to go head-to-head with Carson and put *The Joey Bishop Show* on the air in April 1967. It ran weeknights in the same time slot as Carson.

I got a call to meet Joey and they hired me right then and there. I was the orchestra leader over three trumpets, three trombones, five saxes, piano, drums, bass and guitar, just the most talented studio musicians you could find. They were following the model of *The Tonight Show* very closely. That's where I met Regis Philbin, who was Joey's announcer and sidekick like Ed McMahon was Johnny Carson's. I was like Doc Severinson, Johnny's bandleader.

Because I didn't go into work until the evening, I had plenty of time to do recording sessions during the day. I won my second Grammy in 1967 for "Up, Up and Away" with the Johnny Mann Singers. Interesting-

ly, the most popular version of this song in the United States was recorded by the Fifth Dimension and they won a Grammy for Album of the Year the same year. The Johnny Mann Singers' version was the most popular in the United Kingdom.

The Joey Bishop Show ran for 640 episodes, with loads of movie and TV people as guests. All of the Rat Pack members came, except Frank Sinatra. There was a memorable night when Sammy Davis, Jr. appeared and he, Regis and Joey had this long discussion about the proper way to wear a Nehru jacket. They were all wear-

Regis Philbin, me and Joey Bishop.

ing them. You can see me off to the side in my coat and tie laughing, but they made it clear to the audience I was too square to carry the jacket off. That didn't bother me at all!

I was introduced every night as "The six-foot-two kangaroo" and I'd leap up and do a sideways kick, just for fun. One night, some wise guy in the stage crew put something slippery on the stage, and when I came out and did my jump, I fell down hard. The audience laughed and I got up and laughed too, but it hurt! I never found out who did it.

Because *The Tonight Show* was based in New York and *The Joey*

Bishop Show was based in Hollywood, we were able to get more of the movie and television people, including great singers and musicians. It was always fun when we had a good musical guest. Every weekday evening at six-thirty I'd go to the ABC Studios on Vine Street to have one run-through with the band and the guest star. The musicians were so good that's all they needed.

One time Jimmy Durante was the guest star. He was more of a co-median than a singer, but he did bring his own music. Someone tipped me off that Durante had a habit of getting the conductor's music and throwing it all over the place just to get a laugh. He came in to the re-hearsal and gave his music to the music librarian – my brother Nick -- and without him knowing, we substituted it for something that wasn't important. When the show started and Jimmy Durante came up and grabbed the music off my stand and threw it up in the air, the audience of course went hysterical but it didn't do any harm!

Mel Tormé was the other way around. He didn't want to cause havoc, he was just really hands-on. He came out at rehearsal, he knew all the guys in the orchestra, they all knew him. He'd give them their scores and the guys sight-read through. Then he'd start giving this detailed critique: "Saxes, when you get to the tutti in measure three, I feel like it could be a little more legato… Brass, when you're making the specs – bop! bop!...You can hit them but blah-blah-blah. Drums, don't make the rims too hard because the brass was loud enough, it's just a little too much…." and on and on.

Finally, one of the trombone players raised his hand and said sort of hesitantly, "Hey, Mel, how's our posture?"

It was just a joy conducting that orchestra. Unfortunately, Joey was not a pleasant person to be around. He was an egomaniac. Luckily for me, he didn't know much about music and I stood off to the side con-ducting where I didn't get much attention from the audience, so he only gave me trouble one time. I was rehearsing the orchestra just like I did for every show and all of a sudden I heard yelling and Joey said, "I'm trying to do a commercial over here!" He huffed off the stage and went back to his dressing room. He never apologized in words, but a couple of weeks later he called me into his office and said if I went down to a certain men's shop, they'd make a nice suit for me. I never went. I just let it die. But that was how he apologized.

Regis Philbin was another story. Regis is one of the nicest guys in the world and the audience loved Regis because he was cute and sweet and funny. Joey was terrible with Regis. After a show I'd hear him yell, "REGIS!" and Regis would go to his office and Joey would chew him out: "I just want you to know I'm the star of this show and you're just the announcer!" Stuff like that. So after that Regis would really dial it down and not do anything to get any laughs. Then Joey would start at him again: "REGIS! You're not contributing to the show, you're just standing around!" Oh, poor Joey. I always felt so bad for Regis!

Regis and I got to be good friends. Five nights a week he'd come sit in my dressing room and we'd talk and laugh. He and his family came up to my house and we'd relax around the pool. We had some good times together. I guess Joey's constant criticism made Regis think he was bringing the show's ratings down, so about the time Johnny Carson moved his show from New York to the NBC Studios in Burbank – right in our backyard – Regis started talking to Joey about quitting on the air. Or at least pretending to quit.

The night Johnny Carson's show premiered at its new location in May 1968, Regis quit on the air. He walked off the set and didn't come back for a week. I filled in with his announcer duties and joking around with Joey, in addition to handling the music. ABC got lots of calls and letters and telegrams from fans who wanted Regis back. So he walked back on one night and the show continued as before.

One evening in the fall of 1969 I was driving to ABC for that night's run-through and the news came on the radio that *The Joey Bishop Show* had been canceled. I knew nothing about it, and heard it on the radio! It was just a shock to me. I still had my session work, but you get used to that regular paycheck from a television show. That was a blow.

These years with Danny Kaye and Joey Bishop were very busy for me professionally and I was somewhat lacking as an attentive husband and father. This book tells about my business and personal failures as well as my successes, and this was one of my failures. Lori and I separated in 1969. I kept living in the house in Chatsworth and I bought a new home nearby for her and the girls. I was near enough to see the girls when problems arose, but I never was a close and attentive father.

I was about to get busier than ever in my career with a new vehicle showcasing the Johnny Mann Singers called *Stand Up and Cheer*.

Chapter Six

STANDING UP AND CHEERING FOR AMERICA

I am a patriotic hamburger about America. I love my country. The late 1960s and early 1970s were a very turbulent time in America because of the Vietnam War. Nobody wanted that war but we were there and we were in it. Young men were being drafted into the military and a lot of protesting was going on about it. The protesters were burning flags and doing anything they could to voice their opinion about what America was doing and why it was wrong. I just got my belly full of the protesting. So I thought, Something should be done about it and the only thing I knew to do was music.

In 1970, a few months after *The Joey Bishop Show* ended, I got the idea of finding some younger singers to perform patriotic song-and-dance routines in hopes of putting together a show. I wrote a few arrangements, both traditional patriotic songs and some of my own work. I got some young people together, ranging in age from their mid-twenties to mid-thirties. Some were family members of the pro singers I had worked with, young people who were just making their way. Then I asked Thurl Ravenscroft if he would join us, because his voice was just so deep and wonderful. Thurl needed more money like Custer needed one more Indian, but he was a very patriotic person too, and he agreed immediately.

I also recruited John Felten, who was another great bass singer who sang with a quartet called The Diamonds.

I had eighteen singers come to North Hollywood to an Episcopal church where I rented the children's Sunday School classroom in the basement. There was a piano in the room and some little tables and chairs. I taught them to perform the arrangements I had written and they sounded really good. I wrote out some speeches to introduce the songs and we started getting a show together. We didn't have a financial backer or any special connections, but we started rehearsing. Then Jerry Frank, who had been the producer of *The Joey Bishop Show*, got involved. A few people came in at our invitation to hear us, and one of them was an agent named Ray Sackheim. He said he'd try to book the show for us.

Ray knew a guy from the Sahara Hotel in Las Vegas whose name was Arvid Nelson. He was the hotel impresario, which means he booked the entertainment acts. He visited, we sang a few numbers with my introductory speeches, and Arvid said, "Can you do an hour of that?" and I said, "You bet your boots!" We were going to Vegas! But even before we appeared at the Sahara Hotel, we had an unbelievable

Pat Nixon, Imelda Marcos and me, on my first visit to the White House

opportunity. Mrs. Ferdinand Marcos was to be a guest at the White House on September 22, and we were invited to perform at a luncheon held in her honor by First Lady Pat Nixon. Mrs. Marcos was serving as her husband's ambassador. He was a big ally of the United States.

At this point, you're probably thinking, Uh huh. What about the shoes? This was years before we knew Imelda Marcos had a thousand pairs of shoes, and when I look at the pictures from the White House appearance now, all I see are some simple, plain shoes peeping out from under her cream-colored dress. She was wearing a long dress, even though this was a day-time event and Pat Nixon was wearing a street-length dress. The Johnny Mann Singers performed a long program of songs, including a medley of contemporary love songs – "Raindrops Keep Falling on My Head" and "Gentle on My Mind" included – and my arrangement of "Dixie." I was really proud to lead them in singing "The Voice of Freedom," my song that was inspired by the assassination of John F. Kennedy.

One of my singers, Marcia D'arcangelo, recalled later that she had been so stunned to see former First Lady Mamie Eisenhower sitting in the front row of the audience that she promptly forgot all her dance steps!

We didn't have much time to bask in the glory of our White House appearance, because we opened the next month in Las Vegas. When I told people about our plans, some of them said, "You're producing a patriotic show for Las Vegas? The prostitution and gambling capital of the world? They'll laugh you off the stage." I wish I could have made them eat their words! The show, called *So Proudly We Hail*, ran for two weeks in October, 1970 in the Congo Room at the Sahara Hotel. We performed to packed houses and never ended a show without getting a standing ovation. At one of the shows, we had our standing ovation, and when the audience sat down, an elderly gentleman stood up and called out, "God bless you, son!" It was Colonel Harland Sanders from Kentucky Fried Chicken in his black bow tie and white suit!

We came back and did a second run a few months later and Ray Sackheim brought in someone from advertising for Chevrolet. That guy saw the show and noted the enthusiastic response, with standing ovations again. He went back and talked to John DeLorean, who was the president of Chevrolet, about sponsoring a television special based on the Vegas show. You may remember something about John DeLorean. He was a corporate maverick at General Motors, and he had developed some best-selling cars, including the GTO and other "muscle" cars. He wore hip clothes, liked to rub elbows with show business folks and was married to a gorgeous fashion model. He loved the concept of our Vegas show and agreed for Chevrolet to sponsor a one-hour special, saying, "Put it on the air!" The result was *So Proudly We Hail* featuring actor Henry Fonda, singer Pearl Bailey and the Johnny Mann Singers.

There were all sorts of bad omens about this special. While we were taping it in California, there was a bomb scare and the whole studio was cleared – except our announcer Alex Dreier. He was stuck up in his sound booth behind the stage and no one thought to tell him what was going on! The show was broadcast the night of February 9, 1971. That morning, a major earthquake in the San Fernando Valley had occurred, destroying two hospitals and killing sixty-five people. Plus, the Apollo 14 astronauts were on their way home after a successful moon landing. There was a lot of news coverage of these major events. Even so, the program got a 56 percent audience share. Apparently, I wasn't the only one who loved my country and wanted to feel good about America.

In addition to the audience response, John DeLorean got letters from Chevrolet dealers all over the country saying they loved the show. That convinced him to agree for Chevrolet to sponsor a weekly television show called *Johnny Mann's Stand Up and Cheer*. The show debuted on September 13, 1971, was owned and operated by CBS, and syndicated around the country. Chevrolet was the title sponsor, and the Johnny Mann Singers sang, "See the USA in your Chevrolet" during each show as the audience watched a blue Chevy driving across a bridge.

Each show began the same. The guest star walked into the spotlight with drums rolling and introduced the show with these words: "Almost two hundred years ago, a remarkable thing happened -- the United States of America. Ladies and gentlemen, stand up and cheer!" Then we sang the theme song I wrote. At the close of the show, I would say, "Always remember..." after which the Johnny Mann Singers sang, "Keep your

The cast of my TV show *Johnny Mann's Stand Up and Cheer*

eye on the grand old flag!" as a giant American flag appeared in the background.

The show formula had several high-energy song-and-dance numbers with the Johnny Mann Singers – who we called "the kids" because they were so young and wholesome – plus me, who wasn't quite so young, and Thurl, who was silver-haired. That's why we called him "Pappy." We had a different guest star each week, beginning with Patti Page. Some really great guest singers joined us, like Della Reese, Lou Rawls, Florence Henderson, Bobby Vinton and Mac Davis. If the guest star could sing at all, they performed a number with the Johnny Mann Singers, and if they couldn't they did some speaking part.

For example, Forrest Tucker recited poetry by Walt Whitman with a chorus of the guy singers in the background. Ken Berry, from *Mayberry RFD*, did a tap dance. We even had Lassie on the show, and the kids sang "I Wish I Had a Puppy." I loved having Lassie as my guest, though it was a surprise to me to learn that Lassie was actually a male dog. Apparently the males are easier to train than the females. I've been accused of being so sentimental I would cry at a drainage ditch dedication, but it really tears me up every time I see the movie *Lassie Come Home*. At the end when Roddy McDowall runs to Lassie, who has made it through all sorts of trials as she crossed a thousand miles of country to return to him, I'm just a puddle. We did a cute publicity shot of Lassie chewing on my trombone while I played. The dog must have thought it was another kind of T-bone!

Lassie didn't appreciate my "bone" playing

Jerry Frank and I produced eighty-six episodes of *Stand Up and Cheer* that appeared over two and a half years. The schedule was pretty grueling, as we shot two half-hour shows a week for two weeks, then took a week off. We worked out of the studio at KTLA, Gene Autry's CBS station in Hollywood. On Monday the cast did a sight-reading with music for the two shows and worked all day polishing that. Tuesday the choreographer came to put the show on its feet, so to speak, and teach the singers all the dance moves. Wednesday morning the orchestra came in for three hours and recorded the music, then the singers arrived Wednesday afternoon and recorded over the instrumental music. On Thursday we had a rehearsal in the morning with all the choreography, then the guest stars arrived to work with us in the afternoon.

On Fridays we did the taping with make-up, costume and guest stars for two shows in front of a live audience. All of the singing was lip synced – except the solos -- but no one was aware of this. The kids knew the music so well no one could tell. They were singing along, of course, but you can't sing and dance without affecting the quality of the sound. The budget for each week's show was $33,333.33. How they arrived at that figure, I don't know. It seems like they would have just rounded it off, doesn't it?

We appealed to a variety of audiences with our guest stars. We had Alex Karras, who had just retired from the Detroit Lions and was starting his acting career. Bobby Goldsboro was a big teen heart throb. JoAnne Worley and Arte Johnson from *Laugh-In* appeared, and Andy Griffith and

Don Knotts came at different times. Some guests appeared several times, like the Lennon Sisters. Each guest star was paid a thousand dollars after the Friday taping. Mickey Rooney was the only one who insisted on getting paid up front – even before the taping. After the Thursday afternoon rehearsal, he said he wouldn't come to the taping unless he got paid right away: "I want the money now." We were all shocked. The person who wrote the checks had gone home for the day by then, but Jerry Frank got the thousand dollars somewhere.

On the other hand, Roy Rogers and Dale Evans came on with their family and they all sang for that thousand-dollar fee. They couldn't have been nicer. They didn't bring Trigger and Bullet, however. A number of comedians came on, including Buddy Hackett, Joan Rivers, Milton Berle, Don Rickles and Totie Fields. And Joey Bishop came on a couple of times. He owed me.

When Jim Backus appeared, everyone knew him as the voice of Mr. Magoo and from playing Thurston Howell III, the millionaire on *Gilligan's Island*. He carried his teddy bear from *Gilligan's Island* and sang "You Gotta Have Heart" with the voice of Mr. Magoo.

Show segment featuring "Mr. Magoo," Jim Backus

THE WHITE HOUSE

WASHINGTON

August 13, 1973

Dear Johnny:

Mrs. Nixon and I were delighted that you and all of the Johnny Mann Singers could be with us on June 18 at the State Dinner honoring Secretary General Brezhnev.

Because we wanted the Secretary General to have the opportunity to hear some typical American music, we decided that Johnny Mann and his group were a perfect choice for providing us with enjoyable, "upbeat" musical entertainment. The response of our guest of honor and all our other guests to your splendid performance indicates that we made a wise decision, and we just want you to know how very much we appreciate all that you and the Singers did to insure that the evening would be such a successful one.

With our thanks and warmest good wishes to you and each member of your group,

Sincerely,

Richard Nixon

Mr. Johnny Mann
5800 Sunset Boulevard
Hollywood, California 90028

Appreciation letter from President Richard Nixon

Although *Stand Up and Cheer* was a patriotic show, we performed all sorts of music, including American folk songs, Broadway and movie themes and popular contemporary music. It's kind of painful to watch the videos of the show these days because of the clothes. The main show that sticks out in my memory was the one with mimic Rich Little. Not because of him – though he did a number of his great impressions, including one of me -- but I'm wearing light blue pants, a light blue shirt and white shoes. I didn't hate the shoes at the time. I didn't know how unforgiveable they were. But we wore what the wardrobe guy gave us. A lot of polyester!

In the spring of 1973, we were invited back to the White House. Richard Nixon was still president, and on June 18th he was hosting Leonid Brezhnev, the general secretary of the Soviet Union's Communist Party. It was the first state visit by a Soviet leader since 1959. The White House wanted to showcase patriotism, and they could have gotten any entertainer they wanted to appear, including Bob Hope or Frank Sinatra or anyone else, but they picked the Johnny Mann Singers. It was a real shock, and a great honor. I got to eat dinner with all the guests at the state dinner, after which the cast and I performed.

We did some of the same music we had for Mrs. Marcos, concluding with "Dixie" and "Battle Hymn of the Republic." But as I told you in the introduction of this book, Brezhnev seemed more interested in the girls' short skirts than in the music.

The summer to come was the beginning of the end for President Nixon, as the Watergate hearings started in the Senate after Brezhnev departed for Moscow. He would be out of his job by the next August, but I would lose mine even sooner. I don't know if it was because of the resignation of John DeLorean from Chevrolet in 1973 or just the mood of cynicism that prevailed after the Watergate hearings, but the patriotic feeling in the United States was definitely fading and *Stand Up and Cheer* went with it. Our last show aired January 28, 1974. Nixon resigned August 9, 1974.

Stand Up and Cheer

Stand up and cheer, now is the time we should be heard,
Stand up and cheer, the time has come to spread the word.
This is the land where every man can choose the song he sings,
This is the land where every day the bell of freedom rings.
Stand up and cheer, we must be there when honor calls,
Stand up and cheer, we must reach out to him who falls.
Here is a hand, here is a heart,
Here is a land that we hold dear.
Stand up and cheer, stand up and cheer, stand up and cheer!"

Theme for the television show *Stand Up and Cheer*, words and music by
Johnny Mann, ASCAP, 1971

Chapter Seven

BECOMING A CHRISTIAN MANN

The early 1970s brought some professional highs for me, but some personal lows. I lost my parents, Ells and Lil, within eleven days of each other in 1972. Ells had been ill for some time, but Lil's death was unexpected.

Ells and Dorie, his fourth wife, had come out to California with their daughter Jo some years before. As in Baltimore, Ells worked as a carpenter and at other odd jobs. And as strange as it may sound, almost every Sunday afternoon, Ells, Dorie and Jo came over to the house Lil shared with my step-brother Nick, and I

Me with Gail Wenos and her smart dummy, Ezra D. Peabody

would join them. We'd spend the afternoon together, just relaxing by the pool. Lil and Ells were never hostile that I remember, and I really loved that family time.

A few days after Ells died, Lil had a heart attack. She was in the hospital and I went to see her. She was sitting up in a chair, and she was concerned because she had to rearrange her teaching schedule – she was still teaching voice and leading choirs -- and we talked about how I could help her with that. Right after I left, she had another heart attack and died.

So I was still dealing with that sadness even as I went to the White House and enjoyed all the success of the final year of *Stand Up and Cheer*. There's both sunshine and shadow in life all the time.

Even though the show had been canceled, the Johnny Mann Singers were still a popular draw and we performed a number of out-of-town concerts in 1974 and 1975. During that time I was attending the First Baptist Church of Van Nuys and the minister there, the Rev. Jess Moody, introduced me to a wonderful ventriloquist named Gail Wenos. She and her "smart dummy" Ezra D. Peabody joined some of our tours and added their act to the show. I would come out and joke around with Ezra, who always got the better of me. Not very flattering, when you think about it – but the audience loved it!

On one occasion, my singers and I were on the same plane with Lawrence Welk and his performers, going to different venues in Columbus, Ohio. I was sitting in the coach class with my cast, and all of Lawrence Welk's singers and musicians were in coach too, but he had bought a first class ticket for himself. I went up and chatted with him for a while. Once we got off the plane, my cast and I boarded a very beautiful, comfortable tour bus. Then the Lawrence Welk cast was met by these really awful gray buses, with "U.S. Navy" printed on the sides– but he got chauffeured in his limousine! He was famous for being very careful with his money. Up to a point.

I remember another time we were performing at the Orange County Fair in California, one of three opening acts with Bob Hope. Talk about being careful with your money, the first act was the singer Rudy Vallée, who had been a big name in music and the movies in the 1930s and

1940s. He wouldn't spend the money on a back-up band or even an accompanist. Instead, he had a dinky little cassette recorder on this little stand and he'd press down the button and play a piano track that he sang along with. It sounded just awful.

The next act was Michael Landon, who played Little Joe Cartwright on *Bonanza*. He did a sort of Wild West show with some guys in cowboy suits with trick shooting and stunts. We followed that with some of our patriotic numbers, then Bob Hope came out. I enjoyed spending time talking to Bob in his trailer, but it was a long gig, especially having to listen to Rudy Vallée and his tape recorder!

One of the featured performers in *Stand Up and Cheer* was Lynn Dolin. She was also a songwriter who was interested in Christian music. We began to date and consider marriage, even though she was twenty years younger than I was. My friends – some of the same people who had pushed me to marry Lori in 1960 – told me it was a mistake to marry Lynn. But I thought we had enough in common to make it work.

Lori and I had been separated since 1969, and we finalized our divorce in 1974. With the best intentions in the world, I made a huge mistake. I was earning very good money and I thought, as others have in show business, that the success would never end. I told my lawyer I wanted to continue to pay Lori alimony for life. He said I was crazy and advised me against it. As the kind of music I loved became less popular in the face of rock and roll, my income diminished, and it made paying that alimony very hard at times. All I can say is that my intentions were honorable, but what I did was another of my bad decisions.

At any rate, Lynn and I got married in 1975. Lynn was a very dedicated Christian and she urged me to deepen my relationship with God. We attended small group Bible studies together. But it was the invitation of two friends, Bill Cole and Clark Gassman, that led me into serious study of the Bible. Bill was my leading top tenor in the pro recording groups and Clark was the best creative keyboard player and composer I knew. Both were Christian men. We began meeting for weekly Bible study, just the three of us, and I gradually developed a closer relationship with God. It wasn't a Road to Damascus experience for me, but I finally came to realize God is in charge of my life and that Christ is my savior.

With my Christian mentor, Bill Cole

I have to confess something at this point. In addition to leading the Johnny Mann Singers at the White House twice while Richard Nixon was president, I was invited to the Western White House at San Clemente, California. I was standing in line to shake hands with the president beside this very pleasant gentleman. We were making small talk and I had no idea who he was until I heard the announcement, "Rev. Billy Graham? You're next!"

Through Bill Cole I met someone who knew exactly who Billy Graham was. Ralph Carmichael had done a lot of work in show business but he had also composed scores for films for Rev. Graham's ministry. Ralph is still a giant in Christian music, pioneering a merger of hymns with a big band sound. He had a Christian music label and music publishing company, Light Records/Lexicon Music and Bill was his executive producer. I was no longer with the Liberty Records label, so I recorded two albums, *The Church's One Foundation* and *The Four Freedoms* with Ralph's label. Lynn also did a Christian album. I was invited to appear at the Crystal Cathedral with the Rev. Robert H. Schuller on his *Hour of Power* television program and other appearances on Christian talk shows on radio and television.

My closer relationship with God cushioned another tremendous blow, when I found my beloved brother Nick dead at his home in 1976. He had died of a heart attack and he was just fifty-seven years old. I felt like my own heart was broken, because we were so very close.

Lynn and I continued to live in Chatsworth at the house on the hill. After all the busy, busy years, this was a quieter time in my life and career. I started hatching an idea for a series of choral festivals to recognize talented amateur singing groups, from quartets to choirs, an Olympics of choral music. I called it the Great American Choral Festival.

These days, when choral competitions are held across the country and reality television shows like *American Idol* are making stars of unknowns on a regular basis, my idea doesn't seem that fresh. But at the time, it was unusual, and a lot of people jumped on the bandwagon and urged me to move it into operation very quickly. We launched in 1982 without nearly enough advance planning, which I know now was a mistake. It was one of many mistakes I made with the festival, but hindsight is twenty-twenty and at the time I thought I was doing the right thing.

Over the next three years, I would hear some marvelous music from talented people all over the country and make some great friends. I would also lose my shirt – and meet the love of my life.

Chapter Eight

THE GREAT AMERICAN CHORAL FESTIVAL – AND BETTY

The idea of the Great American Choral Festival was to determine the best performances of singing in the country by holding local and regional competitions leading up to a national one. Once the thing got moving, it was like a juggernaut. I had some partners to put it

Kicking off The Great American Choral Festival with one of the wonderful choirs anxious to perform on January 4, 1982 in Pasadena, California.

together – some of whom, frankly, needed full-time jobs – and they urged me to move forward quickly. I also hired a convention and conference consulting firm to help with the logistics. Those folks said I needed more planning time; I should have listened to them. But nevertheless, we launched it in January 1982.

Greyhound and Hilton Hotels came on as major sponsors, and I routinely got up at five o'clock in the morning to make calls to the East Coast trying to line up other sponsors. (That started a rift between Lynn and me – she was a late sleeper and wasn't involved in the choral festival.) I thought it was important to offer some big prize money, even on the local and regional levels, in order to attract lots of participation. That was another mistake. And the third mistake was that I felt I needed big names in music to be adjudicators or judges to gain credibility for the festival. I asked Fred Waring, owner of Shawnee Press, to be the honorary chairman of the adjudicators, and Dr. Charles C. Hirt chaired the panel. Everyone who judged was paid an honorarium, plus all their travel and lodging expenses were covered.

So even though the sponsors gave me big hunks of money, I got rid of it fast. I was Johnny Generosity when it came to my team.

In every city, we needed to rent venues from colleges and universities or civic auditoriums or big hotels, and that required lots of logistics planning. One of the people who worked for the convention consulting firm in the Midwest was a lady named Betty Schulien. She was willing to travel on weekends, so she came to many of the competition sites from the very beginning.

Our "boot camp" was the first festival, on January 4, 1982 in Pasadena, California at the civic auditorium. You can't imagine what performance days were like. On a Saturday morning, we had up to thirty groups, ranging from quartets to chorales of a hundred or more. They all had to get in costume and make-up, do a warm-up, perform two songs (one of them a cappella), then get off stage for the next group. Then they would sit out in the audience and cheer the other performers on. The people who did it just loved it and so did I!

Now, in advertising the festival, we had sent out the word as widely as we could, hoping to attract all sorts of school and community groups.

The very first check we got in the mail was from the Gay Men's Chorus of Los Angeles. I had known many gay people in show business and I never had a problem with them. They are just people. But we were trying to make this a family-oriented event, and in 1982 the AIDS epidemic was just beginning to be known. It wasn't called AIDS then, but had ugly slang nicknames like "gay cancer" and "gay plague." Nevertheless, on the advice of my attorney and following my own instincts, I accepted the chorus's registration and welcomed them to Pasadena.

It was such a good decision! They were wonderful singers and great to have at the festival – all of them courteous, just perfect gentlemen. And they won first place in the adult division. Many years later, when I was living in Palm Desert, the director of the chorus came up to me at a black tie charity event and told me how much it had meant to them to have that opportunity to perform in public. I made a lot of friends from that, and in later festivals we welcomed other gay choruses, like Turtle Creek from Dallas and Windy City from Chicago.

Winning even on the local level meant so much to these singing groups. There was a small choral group from a high school in Priest River, Idaho. The school had no winning sports teams. Their show choir entered one of our local competitions and won their division. After that, they were eligible to go to the regional competition in Salt Lake City. Everyone in Priest River raised the money so they could make that trip. The choir didn't win, but the kids sat in the audience just mesmerized, watching all these great choirs perform. And that gave them the inspiration to go home and work harder at their music. It was very emotional.

And then there was Betty. I don't believe in love at first sight – that's just hot pants when you fall head over heels at the beginning. Betty was and is a very beautiful lady, but it wasn't just her looks that appealed to me. As we worked together, I got to see how good Betty was and I got to know her and respect her. I fell in love with Betty for a multitude of reasons, and realized it was the first time I had fallen in love in my life.

We were both married to others, but her marriage was unhappy and Lynn and I had grown apart. After months of being on the road, I told Betty about my feelings, and I asked her to come to California to work for the choral festival at the home office as tour director. She came out

The Johnny Mann Singers and Players of yester year. Seated left to right: Sue Allen Brown, Clark's friend, Clark Burroughs, June and Eddie Rosa, Peggy and Wil Schwartz. Standing left to right: Loulie Jean Norman, me and Betty, Thurl Ravenscroft, and Bill Brown

in July 1982 and we both decided we needed to end our marriages and commit to each other. This was not at all easy because of the families who were hurt by our actions.

Some of my friends said, "It's your third marriage. How long will that last?" There was a lot of doubt in their minds because I didn't have a great track record. But this time I knew it was for keeps, and I was right. Betty and I were married on August 20, 1983 and will celebrate our thirtieth anniversary this year.

Our wedding was beautiful. Betty wore a knee-length cream and white dress and I wore a white tux with, yes, white shoes. Her daughter Stephanie was her maid of honor. The ventriloquist Gail Wenos came with her "smart dummy" Ezra, who behaved himself for a change!

Betty inspires me in so many ways it's hard to put into words, but I tried by writing her a poem about my feelings for her. I gave it to her nicely framed and every time I see it, I am reminded of how emotional I felt at its conception.

My love for you is…immeasurable.
It fills my heart, it calms my fears.
It gives me courage when I could falter.
It makes me sing, and it guides my
hand when dreams fade to reality
and I reach for the light.

The greatest gift my Lord has given
me is you. And when He calls me,
the last joy in my life that I take
with me will be…my love for you.

I mean every word of that poem. Meeting and marrying Betty are the greatest blessings of my wonderful life.

Leonid Brezhnev, President Richard Nixon and me at the White House, 1973

Co-hosting the Arthritis Telethon with Jane Wyman

The controversial original cover of my first album, *Night,* in 1956

Christmas with The Chipmunks, Vol. 2

Playing at the Bogie Busters Celebrity Golf Tournament

Palm Springs officials help me unveil the Star

My Star presented by Jackie Lee and Jim Houston of Palm Springs

Me with Harpo The Clown and Dennis James at the Breath of Life Celebrity Golf Tournament that I chaired

Johnny Mann visits Jim Clancy and the Vocal Majority at their Christmas Show - Eisemann Performance Center, Dec. 5, 2008

My favorite men's choral group, The Vocal Majority, led by my good friend, Jim Clancy

My daughters, Jennifer and Susie, visiting me on one of the shows.

Previous Pages:

Leading the All-American College Orchestra at Walt Disney World

On the White House lawn in 1970

Our home in Palm Desert, California

Anderson musical friends Bob and Carla Heritage, Debbie and Gene Rowell, and Jeanine and Doug Douglas

John Myrick
officiated on
August 20, 1983

Me as an army soldier

Framed picture and music from Anderson University commemorating the launch of the Centennial Alma Mater

Receiving my honorary degree from Anderson University. Can you believe Dr. John Mann!

Road Show group, 1987

Chapter Nine

ON THE ROAD AGAIN

The first year of the Great American Choral Festival ended in Philadelphia, the prize money was awarded, and Betty, our team and I were working on the second year. But when I had gone back to Hilton and Greyhound and many of my other sponsors, they told me they

Honorary Mayor of Chatsworth, California

had already committed to sponsoring the 1984 Olympic Games, which were being held in Los Angeles.

I then appealed to my old friend Jerry Henderson, the successful businessman from Las Vegas with the underground homes. Jerry loved the festival and made a sizeable loan so we could keep going. Our understanding was I would pay him back once I got over the funding hump caused by the Olympics. Unfortunately, Jerry died in November 1983, and it wasn't long before I discovered his business associates weren't as understanding about the time table for repaying the loan. I didn't have the money because we had spent it on the choral festival. So they sued us, trying to take our home and land in Chatsworth to repay the loan.

The festival ended in 1984. Betty and I, though we were newlyweds and so happy with each other, entered a very difficult period. The lawsuit

An extraordinary fan from Sweden, Erich Andre, with his albums.

was hanging over our heads all the time. I had lived in that house for more than twenty years and I loved it and Chatsworth. I had been the honorary mayor of Chatsworth since 1982, riding in parades and cutting ribbons. Betty and I even visited the firemen at the firehouse for lunch and went to their parties. To think I would have to leave that wonderful community was so sad.

To make matters worse, there was little session work for me at that time. The kind of music with the back-up singers like mine wasn't being done as much – it was all rock and roll or disco. We tried to trust in the Lord and just wait patiently for something to happen to make things better.

And even in this dark time, some wonderful things happened. In 1986, the Swedish Choral Directors Association invited me to be their guest for a week. Choral singing was so popular then that seven out of

A patriotic hamburger - even in Sweden!

ten Swedes sang in organized choirs. Unfortunately, I came down with the flu and almost didn't get to go, but my fever broke and my doctor gave me his okay to go. We had these big bags – without wheels – and poor Betty was schlepping them into the airport. Fortunately, they flew us in business class and I could stretch out and sleep the whole way.

They had all sorts of festivities that week, including a big concert where I was among the people being honored. I almost lost it when the mass choir on the stage started singing some songs and all the hundreds of people in the audience joined in – in four-part harmony! Can you imagine thousands of people singing these beautiful songs in four-part harmony? I just broke out in tears. I still hear from fans in Sweden from time to time, including a man from Stockholm who has collected thirty-two of my forty records. By the time we were ready to go home, I was finally ready to eat. Betty took my picture by a "hamburgare" sign at a restaurant, because I'm such a patriotic hamburger!

That same year, I got a call from Columbia Artists Management. They asked me to put together a touring company of young singers and dancers to perform a ninety-minute program in venues around the country. We were just thrilled and set to work!

The Johnny Mann Singers from my television show had long ago moved on to other things, so I auditioned an entirely new cast to be the Johnny Mann Singers and Dancers. The eighteen guys and girls we hired were experienced performers who had appeared at places like Disney World and Knott's Berry Farm. The youngest was an eighteen-year-old girl but most of the others were in their twenties. We cast them, choreographed the show, got costumes fitted and made and Betty went to work on the logistics, lining up hotels in all the tour cities.

We did some of my standard numbers, ending each show with "It's a Grand Old Flag" as we had on *Stand Up and Cheer.* We did Broadway and Disney numbers too, including a medley from *A Chorus Line.* The girls wore lots of sequins and shiny satin and, since this was the 1980s, they had really big, permed hair. The guys and I

Stand Up and Cheer Singers/Dancers on the 1989 road tour

still wore those white shoes, but because the dancing was much more athletic, I didn't perform most of the numbers with the cast. I would introduce songs and conduct and sing on a few.

We traveled from place to place on a Greyhound bus. These kids were so much younger than Betty and me that we felt like road parents. The cast was very talented and great on stage, but off stage was something else again. They weren't always very responsible and needed a lot of herding!

One of our favorite road stories was the girl who lost one shoe.

Betty and I got everyone on the bus one morning, we rode all day, and once we reached our next venue and were getting ready for that night's show, this girl came to us all in a panic about her costume. "I'm missing a shoe. I think it's still at the hotel where we were last night!" she said. Betty got on the phone, got the hotel to promise to mail the shoe to our next venue, and then a girl with an extra pair of shoes that were close to the right size loaned them to the girl with the missing shoe.

All kinds of things got left behind, but that was the only shoe, thank goodness. Betty found herself repairing costumes and going to the laundromat a lot to wash them, in addition to her usual logistics planning. I don't know what I would have done without her.

The venues where we played ranged from really nice auditoriums to very old opera houses where players had entertained audiences for a hundred years. We carried our own sound and lighting equipment, which was a good thing because sometimes we'd walk into a theatre and find a single light bulb hanging from the ceiling!

Our sound man was a very talented twenty-one-year-old guy named David Steele. He could do just about anything, including repair the bus on occasion. As in *Stand Up and Cheer*, none of the singing was live except the solos. We even had the kids wear fake microphones on their clothing so the audience had no idea it was all on tape. On the other hand, David was a very independent young man who didn't like to follow rules and conventions. One day he got on the bus wearing a T-shirt that said "Sh- - happens." I gave him a talking to, explaining he couldn't wear something that reflected badly on me and the show. So he changed clothes. I can't remember what the new T-shirt said, but it was even worse than "Sh- - happens."

Our tour lasted nine weeks and we did five to six shows a week, most of them one-night stands. I'd like to say I really enjoyed seeing the country, and much of the scenery was beautiful, but it was also nerve-wracking. Sometimes we cut it really close making it to the next show on time, and once our bus completely gave out and had to be replaced. We were so worried we wouldn't made it we called ahead to warn the local people. As it turned out, a basketball tournament was going on in the venue, and we had to wait once we arrived to set up.

One of the places we stayed for two nights was New Orleans, and that was another story we'll never forget. We had a very talented featured dancer named Bambi in our cast. She had a boyfriend her parents didn't exactly approve of, and seeing that we had a layover in New Orleans, she arranged for him to meet her there. They went out and got married and she quit the show, just like Baby June in *Gypsy*! For us that meant a frantic period moving an understudy into her role and re-choreograph-ing the entire show with one less girl.

Still, the tour was fun when it worked. We got very close to some of our cast members. Most of the guys were gay, and it broke our hearts a few years later to learn that one of them had died of AIDS. Betty also came to depend on Dink O'Neal, a very responsible young man who had a young wife. Dink's wife was studying nursing and he went on tour because they needed the money. He was a great help to Betty. Dink is now the father of three daughters and still in show business and we stay in touch.

We had another great boon from out of the blue when Daihatsu Auto Company contacted a friend of ours in the insurance business. They were launching their auto sales in America and needed a big red-white-and-blue entertainment program for a dinner they were holding in Los Angeles. The show would take place two days after the tour ended and it paid a hefty seventy-five thousand dollars.

I worked with our kids while we were on the road to tailor the show a bit, including a new song I wrote, "Welcome to the World of Daihatsu," and an arrangement of Neil Diamond's "They're Coming to America." We performed the show at the Century Plaza Hotel. I did have to edit one of my speeches, the one that introduced the armed forces medley. I left out the reference to Guadalcanal, figuring it wouldn't sit too well with the Japanese executives in the audience.

Then Betty and I went home and collapsed. While we are resting, I'm going to tell you some of my favorite golf stories.

Chapter Ten

GOLF – OF COURSE!

I started playing golf shortly after I came to California and had enough money to pay for lessons. And was no longer living in a carport, of course. To me it's the only game where you can play all day long and not hit a good shot and then along comes a great shot and that brings you back the next day. I have a good temperament for golf. I've never been one to throw clubs; I just don't get angry at it. No matter how badly I played, I enjoyed being out there on the golf course.

All the musical people I knew played golf. When the Porter Valley Country Club was being built, just a minute away from my home in Chatsworth, I went to meet the general manager. "Boy, we're going to have a lot of good times here," I said to him. "We'll get a lot of new members from the music guys." I started listing them, and one of the people I mentioned was Ray Brown.

"You know Ray Brown?" I asked. "He's the greatest bass player in the world!" The man responded, "Ray Brown? Isn't he black?"

"Yes," I said. He replied, "The company won't allow him to join the club."

"Well, there are fifteen to twenty people I can think of who won't sign up if you won't let Ray Brown in," I told him. And they changed the rules. I wasn't a hero, I just told them the truth. Music people stuck together and we didn't care about segregation rules.

For years I played on Monday mornings with four musician friends. They were Willie Schwartz, the very talented and funny woodwinds player I mentioned before; trombonist Bobby Knight; saxophone player Eddie Rosa; and Tommy Tedesco. Tommy was the No. 1 guitar player in Hollywood. He played the theme music to *Bonanza* and anything else with a guitar theme. He was a remarkable player and could sight-read a violin part on guitar.

I belonged to two golf clubs, Porter Valley Country Club and Lakeside Country Club in Toluca Lake, Burbank. All the other guys in my group belonged to other clubs, so we could play at different courses as each other's guests. Most often people played as foursomes, but we worked out a system to have five players and still form teams. Each guy would take a ball and drop it on the ground. The two closest balls were a team. The other three players became three two-man teams. Talk about a mathematical nightmare as we kept track of all the bets, for of course we made it "interesting." In fact, we bet as individuals and as teams. Everyone had legitimate handicaps and we always played exacting Professional Golf Association rules. We played seriously, but it was all honest and so much fun. Even the really serious players stopped just short of murder in order to win.

One misty morning we were playing at Lakeside Country Club. We were on the third hole when it started to rain, an honest-to-goodness rain. Somebody said, "Should we stop now?" and Willie said, "No, I'm down two and I gotta get my money back!" and someone said, "Well, when do we stop?" and Tedesco replied, "When the rain gets up to Johnny Mann's knees, we quit!"

Another time, Bobby had a two-foot putt, and just missed the hole. The ball was right on the edge of the cup and Bobby was so mad he stalked over and hacked it off the green. Tedesco casually said "Five!" Bobby had to chip and putt it back to make the hole. He took a nine.

Most of our wives played also, and I would put together weekend golf outings for couples to the "Poor Man's Pebble Beach," Sand Piper Country Club outside Santa Barbara. I'd rent a bus and we'd meet on a street corner in the San Fernando Valley. There was always a lot of partying and we'd play on Saturday and Sunday. Peggy Schwartz, Wil's wife and one of my pro singers, was known among the wives to be very forgiving and fun. If a woman got a score over ten on a hole, she'd say, "That's a nine, we don't record double digits."

Even during the really hard times when we were fighting the lawsuit and fearful of losing our home, I could go to the golf course and play and forget the troubles for a while. Betty would go with me and enjoy riding in the cart or walking on the course. I needed all the support I could get!

At the same time our financial problems were easing up, I was invited more and more often to play in celebrity tournaments. Most of these were charity events sponsored by major corporations. I played in the Frank Sinatra Celebrity Invitational fourteen times in Palm Springs, as well as the Andy Williams Tournament in San Diego and several tournaments for the Warner-Lambert Pharmaceutical Company. Over the years, I got two holes-in-one at these tournaments, but I didn't win a car. Once I won a really nice customized golf bag with my name embroidered on it, and another time I won a very expensive set of Mizuno golf clubs. I said I would get them re-sized for Betty, because if the golf clubs I was using were good enough to get a hole-in-one, I didn't need to switch. But really, a

Me with Woody Woodbury and Bo Schembechler

Partner in the practice round, Johnny Lujack

hole-in-one is comprised of a good shot and a lot of luck!

At a cocktail party in Palm Desert, where we were visiting for the weekend, I was approached by a man named Cy Laughter – pronounced like "daughter" – from Dayton, Ohio. He said, "John, I've been looking for you. I want to invite you to my annual Bogie Busters tournament in Dayton." Cy owned a tool and die company that was a major sponsor of the tournament and he had to invite you personally. He and his wife Audrey knew an amazing range of celebrities in the worlds of entertainment, politics, business and sports. His guests for the two-day tournaments included entertainers such as Bob Hope, Peter Marshall, Glenn Campbell, Minnie Pearl and Charlie Pride; politicians such as Speaker of the House Tip O'Neill, George H.W. Bush, and Richard Nixon; and sports figures like Johnny Bench, Don Shula, and Paul Brown (for whom the Cleveland Browns are named).

Once Betty and I got on a crowded bus to get to the golf course and a man in a golf cap graciously gave her his seat. She was bowled over when he introduced himself as Melvin Laird -- the secretary of defense.

Pro basketball Utah Jazz player Mark Eaton made me look short!

I felt like a little kid one day when my golf partners were the great Notre Dame football player and Heisman Trophy winner Johnny Lujack, GOP Minority Whip Rep. Bob Michael and Bo Schembechler, head football coach at the University of Michigan. (By the way, I later discovered that Bo was my son-in-law's first cousin, once removed!)

Bogie Busters was lavish, fun, and Cy spoiled us rotten. We didn't spend a dime. We'd fly into the airport and we wouldn't see our bags until we got to the hotel. All the meals were wonderful, and Baskin-Robbins set up an ice cream bar in the hotel lobby where you could get any of their flavors 'round the clock. At Bogie Busters, Warner Lambert and Frank Sinatra tournaments we would be given golf shoes, shirts, sweaters, golf equipment – you name it. I have a closet full of clothes from these tournaments that I wear all the time. All the celebrities on the circuit joked that we could open our own pro shops with these gifts.

Me with *Laugh-In*'s Paul Keyes

At another tournament I was fortunate to meet Paul Keyes, the writer and executive producer of *Laugh-In*. What a wonderful and creative man -- a real Boston Irishman who had values, ethics and patriotism in abundance. Because he and I hit it off immediately, Paul put us on the list for invitations to the *All-Star Party for 'Dutch' Reagan*, the one for Frank Sinatra and also Clint Eastwood's. These were tapings for a future television broadcast and the audience of all-star entertainers relaxed over beverages before the dinner and festivities for the honoree. This was one black tie event that we really looked forward to. Paul and his wife invited us to watch a Dodgers game once a year when he had the tickets given to him by Frank Sinatra to occupy his box. They were great seats and we had great fun with popcorn, peanuts and hot dogs. Go Dodgers!

As a side note, I had never watched *Laugh-In* during its original broadcasting. I guess I was just too busy to catch much TV. But I got some tapes and watching *Laugh-In* was a treat, even years after it went off the air. Through that show, because of Paul's exceptional comedy writing, I got a new appreciation for many of the former cast members I had met playing golf, like Arte Johnson. Another former cast member became a friend through comedian Woody Woodbury in my "golden" years. He was Dave Madden, who also had the role of the long-suffering

My great buddies Burton "Bubba" Gilliam and Alvy Moore. Can't believe the fun we had!

manager on *The Partridge Family*. Dave is still making me laugh with his daily creativity on emails!

Two celebrities who were very close personal friends over the years were Alvy Moore and Burton "Bubba" Gilliam. Alvy was best known as the slow-witted county agent Hank Kimball on the comedy series *Green Acres*. He and his wife Carolyn traveled to many out-of-town celebrity golf tournaments with Betty and me and lived nearby once we moved to the California desert. Alvy was quite the comedian, and was often featured in entertainments that were part of the tournaments. We miss Alvy and Carolyn, but know they are together again in heaven.

Bubba is most famous for his role as the cowboy foreman with the huge toothy grin in the movie *Blazing Saddles*. Director Mel Brooks "discovered" him in his hometown of Dallas, where he was working as a fireman. He also appeared in *Paper Moon* and many other movies and television programs. Besides being a great golfer, Bubba still appears as a cowboy in television commercials in Dallas. His toothy grin still delights us, and he and his wife Susie remain friends today. We enjoyed many golf trips together and one memorable vacation in Hawaii.

I continued to play and sometimes chair golf tournaments for many years, but over time my game declined. At one of my last tournaments, benefiting Jane Wyman's favorite charity the Arthritis Foundation, I said, "Be sure to put me with guys who don't feel like they have to win." I was part of a foursome of guys in their late seventies and early eighties, all very jovial, and we had a great day. It's customary when you take a potty break to talk about your scores with other members of other teams. They were bragging that they were twelve under par or ten under and someone asked me how we were doing. "Fifteen," I said. The guy was taken aback. "You could win!" he said. "No," I said, "Fifteen *over* par." We could barely par a hole, much less win anything!

I adopted "The Motto of the Lesser Player: It was a good shot if you could find it." These days playing golf is just a memory – but what a great memory it is!

Chapter Eleven

MATTERS OF THE HEART

After that refreshing interlude on the links, it's back to our story. By 1988, Betty and I knew we were going to lose our home and land in a court judgment and were worried about where we would live. The housing market in California was crazy at the time. People were not only paying the full asking price for homes, they were in bidding wars above the asking price. One day we were eating lunch at a Chatsworth restaurant and our Realtor Helen Trembicki came over dangling a set of keys. She said, "I just found your house."

Helen had just previewed a home on a cul-de-sac in a typical Chatsworth neighborhood. We walked right out of the restaurant with her, went to see the house and offered the asking price that day. It was quickly accepted. It was not a special home, but it had just what we needed – an office and a guest room and all sorts of storage. At least we had the pressure off of us to go out and house hunt and we moved right out of the big house into that one. Still, for me it was emotionally terrible because I loved that big old house.

In 1989 we did another nine-week tour for Columbia Artists Management with the Johnny Mann Singers and Dancers. We had a mostly

Northridge Hospital Medical Center's "Steppin' Out" fundraiser. Seated, Betty, me and Judy Keel. Standing, Don and Peggy Porter, Howard Keel, June and Eddie Rosa.

new company, though Dink O'Neal returned and was so helpful, and our free-spirited sound/light/bus repair guy David Steele. We had two performers who walked out on the show in Baltimore, and as you can imagine, losing people on the road is not wonderful. You can't hire and fire people on the road, you have to reconfigure the show on the fly and keep going. I was sixty years old by then and came home pretty worn out, just in time to have a heart attack. Betty believes the constant stress of that tour contributed to it.

We regularly walked at Northridge Mall. I have such long legs and walk so much faster that I would walk in a zigzag rather than leave Betty in the dust. One day I got so short of breath I could barely keep up with her. I didn't have an elephant-on-my chest feeling, but Betty called our doctor and he sent me to the emergency room at Northridge Hospital. They immediately administered a clot-busting drug in an IV and told me, "John, you're having a heart attack." In ten minutes I felt fine and said I was ready to go home, but they kept me a while, then I began cardiac rehab as an out-patient.

Studio singers in LA: Bob Joyce, Randy Crenshaw, Don Shelton, me, Melissa Mackay, Darlene Koldenhoven & Linda Harmon

This was the beginning of a wonderful relationship with Northridge Hospital. We both volunteered at the hospital – Betty in the auxiliary and I on the foundation board – and Betty eventually went to work in the medical staff office. She handled continuing education for the doctors, their annual retreat and Christmas party, and really enjoyed that. I would drive Betty to work in the morning, stop in the medical staff lounge for a bagel and visit with the docs, maybe do cardiac rehab, then go on about my day and pick her up after work.

After that last experience with the kids on the road, I knew my touring days were over. Then another wonderful thing happened. A man I had known in the early 1960s when I wrote a few radio jingles called me. His name was Bill Drake. I had gotten out of the jingle business for a long time because of rules imposed by

Studio singers in Nashville: Gary Pigg, Lisa Bevill, Engineer Brent King, Bonnie Keen-King, me, Rod Fletcher, Mark Ivey, Melodie Crittendon-Kirkpatrick

UniHealth American Singers with David Van Gorder in his chair

the American Federation of Television and Radio Artists, the labor union for on-air talent. Broadcasters like to use a jingle several times an hour all day long. AFTRA imposed a rule that the stations had to pay all the talent again after a jingle ran for thirteen weeks. Well, no station wanted to do that. Some jingle companies were operating in Texas using non-union talent and generating jingles very cheaply. The quality wasn't as good, and, unfortunately, they even stole some of the jingle melodies I had written. I thought about suing, but an attorney advised me against it, saying I'd never get anything out of it. AFTRA finally realized they were cutting the performers' throats with the thirteen-week rule and dropped it.

Bill Drake knew of me from my work for KHJ-Los Angeles, where I had done the a cappella jingle when the musicians' union was on strike. Bill had become very successful as a radio station consultant, and he wanted his clients to use a Johnny Mann jingle package. We met and got to be friends. Bill booked the first package and it was like we were happily married! He'd give me an order for twenty jingles, I'd record them with my pro singers in Los Angeles, and word-of-mouth spread in the industry that Johnny Mann jingles were the way to go. It was like a landslide once it started and it was very good money. That filled the big financial hole left by the Great American Choral Festival. I'm still doing some jingle work today, recording both in Los Angeles and with pro singers in Nashville.

I guess it was like I became an elder statesman at this point. People started calling me to do commercials. They ranged from the international charity Feed the Children to Yamaha keyboards. The Feed the Children commercial was extremely successful and stayed on the air for years. I did a lot of guest conducting around the country. For several summers, I was invited to come to Walt Disney World to rehearse and conduct the All-American College Orchestra. This was a summer program Disney ran that brought instrumentalists from all over the country to Orlando for a series of clinics focusing on different types of music. Henry Mancini and Glen Campbell are other music people who worked with them. After a week of rehearsing, we performed a couple of outdoor concerts at Disney's American Pavilion.

It was great working with these very talented young people, but believe me it wasn't easy to conduct two concerts in Orlando in the summer time wearing a suit! In between shows I would go into my air-conditioned trailer so I could change and every item of clothing I was wearing – including my tie! – was soaked with perspiration.

My Yamaha keyboard commercial

Another great opportunity came along when I was invited to Mardi Gras in New Orleans to be the king of a krewe, thanks to Eleanor Vallée, Rudy's wife. The krewes in New Orleans are clubs that put together the floats and throw huge parties before parades, and each of them has a celebrity as a king to ride the float.

White tie and tails at Mardi Gras with the King

Roy and Diane Hollingsworth came with us that week and it was something else. We went to the ball the night before, me in white tie and tails (and white shoes, of course). There was a court of beautiful young ladies, and I escorted the queen down the aisle. From that nice, controlled formal evening, we were out in the street the next day and everybody was going ape, throwing beads and drinking and doing all kinds of other things I won't mention. I was sitting high on the float, just riding along and hoping I didn't fall off.

With Betty working for Northridge Hospital, I found another venue for leading choirs and producing concerts. From 1992 to 1994 I directed a choir of eighty-five health care employees, volunteers and friends in the UniHealth Americans free concert series. It was a public relations choir for UniHealth, a network that included Northridge Hospital. We did a lot of American music medleys, like Cole Porter songs and Disney movie themes and concluded with patriotic songs, always ending with "It's a Grand Old Flag."

One of the people in the choir was Dr. David Van Gorder, a psychologist and counselor. As a young man, he had been in a construction accident that left him paralyzed. He was in a wheelchair and had very limited use of his hands and arms. David sat at the front of the choir in

Let the Games Begin! Shaking hands with California Governor Pete Wilson, right.

his chair, and people would ask him, "David how do you like singing in that choir, sitting right in front of Johnny Mann?" He would reply, "I love it because I love singing. The only negative is with Johnny Mann spitting on me!"

Later on, David and his wife Mary moved to Prescott, Arizona, where they built a house. It was customized throughout to accommodate David's wheelchair, and he came up with most of the design himself. Betty and I went out to visit him several times and always had so much fun. I always enjoyed giving Mary some relief from her regular job of "feeding" Dave his Scotch and soda!

David was the spark behind this memoir, because he asked me lots of questions and recorded them on tape. I like to think I repaid the favor because he had a great desire to paint, but couldn't hold a brush. I told our great friend from Northridge Hospital, Dr. Julio Pro, about him. Dr. Pro is amazing. He is an anesthesiologist but also a gifted painter, classical pianist and Italian cook. Talk about a Renaissance man! He met David and suggested using a sling which could hold a brush between his fingers. It worked, and David has not only produced paintings but has had showings of his work. Dave was another one of those incredible people God put in our path. He accepted his physical limitations and still makes the most out of life.

In September 1993 I had just turned sixty-five, so it's probably fitting that I wrote the official song of the California State Senior Olympics. It was performed by a college choir to open the games in San Diego.

Here are the words:

> *Let the games begin…let the people roar.*
> *We're all gonna give one hundred percent and maybe more.*
> *We're havin' fun…as you can plainly see*
> *Everybody here would say the best is yet to be.*
> *It's a brand new start…and a brand new day.*
> *Just remember that we've got some new friends*
> *showin' us the way.*
> *Let the people shout…that's what this is all about*
> *And we're all together…let the games begin.*
> *Let the games begin…everybody's here*
> *It was meant to be*
> *Surely this will be a special year.*
> *This you won't forget, it's the most exciting yet.*
> *The world is waiting…let the games begin!*
> *Let the games begin…let the games begin!*

Words and Music by Johnny Mann, ASCAP, 1993

For Betty and me, some wonderful golden years were ahead. But first, we had to shake, rattle and roll a bit.

Chapter Twelve

ALL SHOOK UP

At 4:31 a.m. on January 17, 1994, an earthquake shook the San Fernando Valley, with Northridge at its epicenter. Fifty-seven people died and damages were in the neighborhood of twenty-five billion dollars. It was one of the most expensive natural disasters in our country's history. We were spared, by the grace of God.

The Northridge Hospital where Betty worked was heavily damaged. We were at home in bed sleeping when it began. If it had struck a few hours later when Betty was working in her office, she'd be dead because all the floor-to-ceiling files surrounding her desk came crashing down. We came to see her office the next day and cried to think what would have happened. In our house, my grand piano in the living room rolled across the pile carpet, then rolled back

Betty, me and our friends Howard and Judy Keel

Outdoor concert at Del Webb Sun City, with Peter Marshall performing
with the band

and slammed against the wall. (One of my Grammy awards fell and
broke. Someone asked me if I was going to get it repaired and I said,
"No, I've got another one.")

My old house on the hill, the one we had lost in the court case, was
damaged so heavily it could not be saved. The cathedral ceiling caved
in. It became clear to me why I had left that house for a smaller but
safe one. God took us out in time.

Some of our neighbors' homes were heavily damaged, and we all
went without water for more than a week. We bought water to drink and
dipped water from a neighbor's pool to fill our toilet tanks. The earthquake pulled the neighbors together. In the late afternoon, people
brought out barbecue grills and food and we cooked out. It was like a
big block party every night! A musician friend of ours, Ed Lojeski, had
power and water so we went to his house a few times to take showers
and get a hot meal.

That's when I started getting itchy to move to the desert. Palm
Desert is about an hour and a half from L.A., one of a number of
communities surrounding Palm Springs in the Coachella Valley. I co-

owned a condo in nearby Indian Wells with my Bible study friend Bill Cole. We had visited Del Webb Sun City in Palm Desert, a gated community for people fifty-five and over, and we liked all that was there. It's gorgeous, it's warm, it's dry. We wanted to get out of the L.A. traffic. We'd gotten to be close friends with the actor and singer Howard Keel and his wife Judy and many more people who lived there. Plus there are more than a hundred twenty-five golf courses in the Coachella Valley.

It seemed like a good time to move. So many people needed temporary housing while their homes were repaired after the earthquake that we rented our Chatsworth home over the next two years to three different couples we knew through Northridge Hospital. That gave us a steady source of income to move to Palm Desert. We bought a lot and started building a house in Del Webb Sun City and meanwhile borrowed a condo in Palm Springs from our good friends Roy and Diane Hollingsworth.

Living in Palm Desert was very different from L.A., which is packed with big stars. In the desert I was a bigger star than I was in L.A.—but in a very small galaxy. As soon as we moved, we got involved in the social scene. So much money is concentrated in that area, like in Palm Beach in Florida, because of all the retired corporate executives as well as show business folks. There were constant golf tournaments, galas, dinners, luncheons and the like for every cause, including the most "popular" diseases in the world. At the hairdresser's right after we moved, Betty met a very wealthy philanthropic lady named Jackie Lee Houston, who invited us to join her table at an event that weekend. Her husband Jim was a very successful businessman who joked that he had to keep working so Jackie Lee could keep giving away his money!

Fortunately for me, a tuxedo is like a uniform for a musician, so I had the right clothes for these occasions. Betty got very familiar with the consignment shops so she wasn't wearing the same formal dresses every week. She even bought a gown that Ginger Rogers had consigned. Fortunately, she didn't expect me to dance like Fred Astaire when she wore it!

At a golf tournament, I met a talented young actor named Kelsey Grammer, and therein lies a sad tale.

Chapter Thirteen

KELSEY, ME, AND THE CD

When we met in 1994, Kelsey Grammer was the star of his own television show *Frasier*, playing the uptight psychiatrist Dr. Frasier Crane. *Frasier* was a spinoff from the long-running show *Cheers*. His show was doing great, but it was a very stormy time in Kelsey's life. He had women problems, drinking problems, drug problems, you name it. He kept winding up on the front page of *The National Enquirer*.

We met at a celebrity golf tournament dinner. I had heard him sing a little something on *Frasier*, and I said, "You know, Kelsey, you've got quite a voice. You should make a CD." Kelsey said, "I have always wanted to! Let's talk." I didn't hear from him for a couple of weeks, then a friend called me up and said, "I was just watching *The Arsenio Hall Show* and he had Kelsey Grammer on. Arsenio asked him what he was up to and he said, 'I'm making a CD with Johnny Mann.'" So I said, "I'd better call him."

Kelsey's life had been very dramatic and very sad. His father had abandoned his family and later was murdered. His father had a second family and two of his half-brothers drowned. His only sister Karen, who he loved very much, was raped and murdered by serial killers in Colorado. Because of all the trouble he kept getting into, a lot of people didn't realize Kelsey was very intelligent and hugely talented. He had been trained at the Julliard School in acting, had appeared in numerous Shakespeare plays and in the musical *Sunday in the Park with George.*

I called him, confirmed that he wanted to do the CD with me, and chose ten wonderful old standards for him to sing. Rod Stewart had just done that and it had been a big hit. Kelsey had a smooth baritone voice and I chose ballads that would work well with it. Some of them were "Softly as I Leave You," "In the Still of the Night," "I Wonder Who's Kissing Her Now," and the World War II song "(There'll Be Bluebirds Over) The White Cliffs of Dover." I wrote a song about his sister Karen for him to sing, but he got so emotional he just couldn't do it. He was still grieving her loss very much.

Kelsey was paying for the whole project and money was no object. He paid for me to work with Billy Byers, a first-rate orchestrator. I put the vocal arrangements together and Billy orchestrated all of them and we brought in a full orchestra to back Kelsey in the studio. When we did the session, I conducted and Kelsey stood there and listened. Later we went in the sound booth. We both wore headsets and I conducted him singing over the music.

At that time he was suffering through some romantic problems and he puddled a couple of times doing the very poignant love songs. But he would start again and the finished CD was just beautiful. I was so proud of it! I tried to get some record companies interested, but they only wanted pop and rock stars who would be releasing multiple CDs. They didn't want a one-time shot, a novelty like *Dr. Frasier Crane Sings the Oldies.*

Eventually, I arranged for Kelsey to sell the CD himself through television commercials and a toll-free number, and even had booked a studio for him to make the commercial. That's when he told me his girlfriend, who was much younger, didn't want him to release it because, she said, "No one likes those old songs."

He did perform my arrangement for him of "God Bless America" on a float during the Macy's Thanksgiving Day parade, lip-syncing to the recording. But he put the CD aside and never released it. There are countless people who have heard the master I have and everyone who

Kelsey Grammer recording the gorgeous CD that wasn't released.

has heard it has raved about it.

Kelsey and I had a good relationship for several years. We spent a lot of evenings together and he even nicknamed Betty. He called her "Bean." We went to his wedding a few years later – not to the girlfriend who had convinced him to drop the CD project. He's since married someone else. *Frasier* had an eleven-year run on television, and Kelsey now stars in a show called *Boss*. He does lots of voiceovers, too, but I don't know if he does any singing.

It's not too late, Kelsey! You could release the CD and sell it on iTunes. Call me!

Chapter Fourteen

THE DESERT YEARS: SOCIAL WHIRL AND QUIET TIMES

I don't want to say that Kelsey Grammer's decision not to release his CD broke my heart, but I did start having coronary problems again about that time and underwent triple bypass surgery at Eisenhower Medical Center in Palm Springs. Fortunately, all went well, I was released in three and a half days, and I was soon back to my usual activities.

These included playing in and chairing golf tournaments, guest conducting, recording jingles with my pro singers in Los Angeles and attending many, many charity events with Betty. From 1997 to 2000 I shared emcee duties with Jane Wyman for Arthritis Foundation telethons, and I also chaired a golf tournament for the foundation. You may remember Jane Wyman was a very talented actress and the first wife of Ronald Reagan. She was also very tough and hard-nosed. If you were on her side, you had a great ally. Thank God I was on her side! She became reclusive in later years as her health declined but Betty and I were among the privileged few who she allowed to visit her.

Of course, the best golf tournament in the desert was the Frank Sinatra Celebrity Invitational, which I began playing in long before we moved there. It started as a fundraiser for the Desert Hospital and a charity Frank and his wife Barbara founded for sexually abused children.

Me with the famous Oak Ridge Boys Quartet

Who doesn't recognize Jamie Farr, even without a dress!

Later, all the proceeds went to this Barbara Sinatra Children's Center at Eisenhower Medical Center. Barbara was very hands-on with her charity, unlike many celebrities, and I admired this very much.

The Sinatra tournament was played simultaneously on two different golf courses – meaning a lot of participants. There were dinners and entertainment each night, concluding with a very classy black tie gala at the end of the tournament. In the early years, Frank brought in a big band and sang for his guests. Later, he called on old friends like Tony Bennett to entertain. After the gala, a smaller group of celebrity golfers and sponsors went to a compound at Frank's Palm Springs estate. He had built it in the 1960s for an expected visit from President Kennedy that never happened. There was more impromptu entertainment then. Comedians like Don Rickles would get up and kid around with the audience. They could get loose! It went into the wee hours of the morning, concluding with breakfast. That's where I had my best time, when I sat there with Frank, just chatting. That was a treat.

I did another kind of shooting, too. These days there is a lot of discussion regarding limits on gun ownership. I've very grateful to have been included in the Charlton Heston Celebrity Shoot several times in the 1980s and 90s. This event raised funds for the National Rifle Association to defend the 2nd Amendment and also for the U.S. Olympic Shooting Team. Talk about shooting stars! Many celebrities and sponsors took part, learning about gun safety while shooting pistols, rifles and shotguns at targets and enjoying skeet-shooting as well. It was a thrill for me to hang out with Roy Rogers and his son Dusty, along with a ton of familiar show biz names. We had a great time, and one year I was lucky to win a Smith and Wesson revolver during the competition.

I mentioned Betty meeting a philanthropic lady named Jackie Lee Houston when we first moved to Palm Desert. Every year Jackie Lee and her husband Jim chose someone to honor with a star on the Palm Springs Walk of Stars. The walk was started in 1992 and now 350 stars are embedded in the sidewalks of Palm Springs. The stars recognize people who have homes in the desert communities and have prominence in show business and other fields, like sports and the military. They include Debbie Reynolds, Lucille Ball, Jack Jones and my friend Howard Keel.

The walk is a major tourist attraction for the city.

In 1998, Jackie Lee and Jim selected me for this honor. They sponsored the star and invited 400 of my "closest" friends to a big gala at their home. The Houstons didn't do anything half way! Everyone was instructed to wear red, white and blue. They hired musical groups, magicians, a guy in an Uncle Sam costume who walked around on stilts. They even brought in a high school marching band and cheerleaders! A lot of my pro singers from the early days, including Peggy Schwartz, Sue Allen and Bill Brown, came to the party and we got up on the stage and sang "Dream" a cappella. It was a really special night.

A very tall Uncle Sam greets us at the Houston Estate.

Jackie Lee and Jim were incredibly generous with their money, and she just loved being a hostess. She chaired countless charity events. Jim was just a sweet, nice guy who loved making her happy. She died a few years ago of complications from pancreatic cancer and they flew the flags at half-mast in Palm Springs. It just shows you can have all the money in the world and you can't always fix a serious health problem.

In 2001, I was chosen as the subject – make that the victim! – of the American Cancer Society Celebrity Roast. Once again, many of my old friends and new ones came to give me a hard time about different things. Howard Keel was one of the speakers. Howard, his wife Judy, Betty and I went to all these gala dinners and benefits and Howard and I played a lot of golf. Whenever I'd do something silly on the golf course, he'd call me a certain two-syllable naughty name. Then when we were at a fancy dress event in tuxedos, he'd clean it up a bit and call me "Ethel" instead. He kept calling me "Ethel" during the roast and anyone who played golf with us knew what he was really saying, and the others probably really wondered about us.

Depending on your age, you know Howard Keel in different ways. In the 1940s he was a successful leading man in stage productions of *Carousel* and *Oklahoma!* Then in the 1950s he starred in a series of big Hollywood musicals, including *Annie Get Your Gun* and *Seven Brides for Seven Brothers*. He appeared in Westerns in the 1960s. But, like me, Howard went through a period when his kind of music wasn't popular and he mostly did touring productions. What brought him back to the public eye was in 1978 when the producers of the television series *Dallas* contacted him. The actor Jim Davis, who had played the series patriarch Jock Ewing, died unexpectedly and they wanted to cast a second husband for "Miss Ellie" Ewing. Howard played Texas oil man Clayton Farlow until the show ended in 1991, and his popularity on *Dallas* revived his music career, too.

The "Roasters" left to right: Johnny Lujack, the Roastee (me), Howard Keel, Diane Marlin-Dirkx, Gordon "Whitey" Mitchell, Bill Marx, Chuck Taylor, Peter Marshall and entertainer Kenny Bob Davis

Even though Howard was from Illinois, he had played in so many western roles that he still dressed the part. I don't have a record of what he said to me at the "massacre," but in my rebuttal I told him, "I've always idolized you, but I just don't have the guts to sport a mustache and cowboy clothes."

To be honest, the funniest comments that night were made by Diane Marlin-Dirkx, who was the fashion columnist at *The Desert Sun* newspaper. She gave me a grooming and fashion critique that makes me cringe to this day. Diane compared my eyebrows to "two fat and happy caterpillars at rest" and my hair to "a frenzied orgy of mating Brillo pads." She told the audience she had it on good authority that I made sure there are creases in my sweat pants and once spent twenty minutes shifting a tube sock from one foot to the other "because it just didn't feel right."

But she really hit below the belt when she made fun of my white loafers. "Give the white shoes the boot or style-wise you may be pushing up daisies," she said, and then she gave me a pair of white shoes with daisies planted in them!

I didn't let these accolades go to my head. My mother taught me well. As a young lad, I was always expected to clear the table after the meal. That was the least I could do for Lil, and the practice stuck with me all my life. Well, in our desert social whirl, we were once invited to a very posh dinner party celebrating a special anniversary. We had enjoyed cocktails and trays of hors d'oeuvres had been passed around, and then the seventeen guests were seated at a lovely dinner table. After eating a first course that I couldn't recognize but which was nonetheless delicious, I pushed back my chair and started to pick up my plate and the one next to me. I was quickly stopped in my tracks by my hostess, who said in a very formal, clipped tone of voice, "John, we have people to do that!" Needless to say, I sat right back down. Lil had done too good of a job.

Betty was seated far away from me at the other end of the table and she had her own problem. The man seated to her right had drunk way too many cocktails and kept groping her knee throughout the meal! It was all she could do not to haul off and stomp on his foot, but she didn't want to make a scene and ruin the party. I had no idea what was

GERALD R. FORD

February 25, 2001

Dear Johnny:

It is my privilege to congratulate you, Johnny Mann, on being honored tonight by The American Cancer Society. You have had a lifelong and legendary career as a composer, arranger, conductor, entertainer and recording star - which has provided enormous enjoyment to people all over the world. Also, your charitable efforts and humanitarian endeavors are an inspiration to us all.

Congratulations on receiving this prestigious recognition and best wishes for a successful evening.

Gerald R. Ford

A congratulatory letter from President Gerald Ford on the occasion of the American Cancer Society Roast

going on until afterward, but I did notice she had a strange expression on her face and got up as quickly as she could after dinner. Maybe our hostess should have had "people" to control overly friendly guests, too!

Not every social occasion was formal or benefiting some charity or another. We had a wonderful hairdresser, David Fogg, and we got to be very good friends with him and his partner David Manwill. We called them the Davids. Once they invited us to their California home near the Mexican border and took us out to a very nice white tablecloth restaurant in Tijuana. It was a Sunday afternoon and as we were sitting there chatting before our food arrived, I noticed a song by the Johnny Mann Singers was playing on the sound system. After that, another one of my songs came on. Then it clicked that the Davids had given *The Best of the Johnny Mann Singers* CD to the restaurant owners to play, just to surprise me. That was the kind of thing they did.

The Davids loved antiques and did a lot of antique hunting. Once for my birthday, they gave me an old hymnal, "Worship in Song." I'm thinking, Oh no, another hymnal, but I opened it and flipped through it, commenting on all the nice old hymns. About half-way through, they had carved out a deep hole at the hymn "I Have Found a Hiding Place" and put a monogrammed silver flask in it! I just howled, and when I pulled the flask out, I saw that the "hiding place" was lined with another hymn, "Revive Us Again"!

Speaking of the Davids, I got a kick out of the older, well-to-do, single women who were looking for eligible males to escort them to the various charity events. Obviously, the gay men of the desert were fine escorts. But many of the women were looking for possible husband material. They had two prerequisites: Mr. Right had to be able to dance and drive at night!

Not everything we did was light and amusing, though. At one social event, I met a warden from a nearby prison and told him, "I've always wanted to go to a prison and put together a male chorus." The warden had his activities director call me, and Betty and I drove out to the prison. We went through all the security and wound up with about thirty guys in a classroom. No guards in the room, and one beautiful female with thirty guys, some of them "lifers"!

Betty later said she wasn't nervous. She figured if these guys were chosen to be in there, they could be trusted. I admit I was a little worried. There was a guy in the front row, a great big black dude with a stocking on his head and a very stern expression on his face. I didn't want him mad at me –but I did want his deep bass voice in my choir!

For the first session, I had written a very simple arrangement of the country song "Elvira." I asked which guys sang high, which guys sang low, and grouped them accordingly. Were they good singers? No! As easy as my arrangement was, they still couldn't learn it. But they had a good time. Several of them came up to us afterwards, thanking us and shaking hands, asking for autographs. One young beanpole of a guy was just covered in tattoos. He told Betty, "I'm going to get Johnny's autograph and I'm going to put it on me!" So somewhere there may be an ex-con walking around with Johnny Mann tattooed on his neck. Or somewhere worse!

After that first day was over, one of the guards told us on the way out, "Do you realize how important that was? Those guys only stick with their own." What he meant was within the prison, the blacks, Asians and Hispanics didn't mix, they wouldn't even sit beside each other. When I had grouped them by voice, those barriers had broken down "See what music can do?" the guard said.

We kept at it, and the next time a couple of guys came in with guitars and I added that to our sessions. Later on they had a ceremony for the men who had earned their high school equivalency degree and asked me to come out and do some music for that. I was in a corner with the piano and the guys with the guitars and one who played drums. It was truly emotional for Betty and me, to see some of these guys in really flimsy black caps and gowns come walking in. A few of them spoke. One kid got us teary because he thanked so many people who helped him get his degree and then held up his diploma and said, "This is for you, Mom!"

Unfortunately, the warden I had met was replaced with a real hard-nosed guy and he did away with all kinds of privileges, including the music program. It was too bad.

Opportunities for spiritual growth continued in the desert. Betty met a woman named Catherine Martin, who is the founder and president of

Quiet Time Ministries. She became active with this and came home from a meeting one day talking about how well Quiet Time was going. "I said, 'Quiet Time,' that's a great title for a song." So I sat down and wrote one. A couple of hours later, I called Catherine up and she came right over and sat on the piano bench while I played and sang it to her. She was so thrilled and excited – even with my voice! We went to L.A. and recorded the song with some pro singers and issued it in an album along with some old gospel music and hymn medleys I had recorded previously. Catherine offers this on her website along with her books and Bible study materials and she even uses part of the song as background music on her blogs and DVDs.

If I had to pick from all my albums for my favorite one, I'd choose *Glorify His Name in Quiet Time* because of the medleys and the Christian theme.

Words and Music by Johnny Mann, ASCAP, 2002

Lyrics of the Song
"Quiet Time"

For me to sing unto my Lord, for me to worship Him,
I only need to be alone in my quiet time.

My thoughts, my prayers are music to my heart,
And I can sing my song to Him in my quiet time.

My Lord, I ask you to take my hand and lead me on a
path of love to be with you.

To live with you through out eternity, revive my heart,
revive my heart, Oh Lord.

And so I pray each day to have you in my heart.
So I can raise my arms in praise, reach unto my Lord.
Sing His holy name – Jesus! He is my Jesus!
I love my Jesus.

He is always there. He is always there in my quiet time.
My quiet time.

Words and music by Johnny Mann, ASCAP

Choral Music Company, ASCAP

I am so blessed by the life and music of Johnny Mann. It is incredible to experience his God-given gift of writing beautiful music in action to glorify the Lord. His new song Quiet Time crystallizes the passion of my heart and life. May the inspiring words of Quiet Time and the other hymns on this album become your prayer and move you near to the heart of God.
Catherine Martin

"In writing the song, 'Quiet Time', The Lord truly used me in His purpose of letting more of the world know about His precious servant, Catherine Martin, President, Founder/Director of Quiet Time Ministries. It is a blessing and a privilege to be working with her."
Johnny Mann

TRUE TO THE RED, WHITE AND BLUE

One of the places Betty and I often took visitors when we lived in the desert was the Palm Springs Air Museum, which has a large display of aircraft from World War II. One of the volunteers there told us of a young school teacher who brought her class to the museum. The teacher explained that all the planes the children were seeing were used in World War Eleven.

Can you believe that? How can a school teacher be so ignorant of our country's history? And how will children ever learn how important the United States has been to the world when they are fed junk like that? Well, maybe she just didn't know what a Roman numeral is.

As I have said before, I am a patriotic hamburger when it comes to my country. Because of *Stand Up and Cheer*, I became widely known for this and received a number of awards and citations from patriotic organizations. These organizations include the American Veterans of World War II, Korea and Vietnam, Disabled American Veterans, Veterans of Foreign Wars, American Legion and Daughters of the American Revolution. The most important to me are the three consecutive George Washington Honor Medals from The Freedoms Foundation at Valley Forge. These are hanging in my home office, beautifully framed.

I've also been fortunate to have met many important people in our government, including four presidents – Richard Nixon, Gerald Ford, Ronald Reagan and George H.W. Bush – and gotten numerous unsolicited letters from them and others who appreciated my patriotic music such as Sen. Barry Goldwater and President George W. Bush. I am including some of these letters in this chapter – just to prove I'm not making all this up!

After the Johnny Mann Singers appeared at the White House, we were invited to perform for Ronald Reagan and his wife Nancy when he was governor of California. Some years later we met again at a fund-raiser. When President Reagan died in 2004, I wrote a song for Nancy called "What You Meant to Me," and sent a recording to her. Here are the words:

We know the joy we feel in laughter,
The smiles we sing in a song,
The love we share forever after,
And the life we live when we belong.
We know that hills surround the deepest valleys
And that streams flow gently to the sea,
But there's no one on earth that could ever know
What you meant to me.
And now you're gone to where there are no fears,
Where you can spread the joy of you across the sky,
And there's the sun to shine away your tears
And send a ray of hope to those who wondered why.
We know that clouds can turn to raindrops
But soon the raindrops are gone.
We know that rain can turn to snowfall
And that dark will surely fade to dawn.
We know that spring will bring the flowers
And that leaves fall gently from the tree.
Ah, but there's one thing that only God can know
What you meant to me.

Words and music by Johnny Mann, ASCAP, 1994

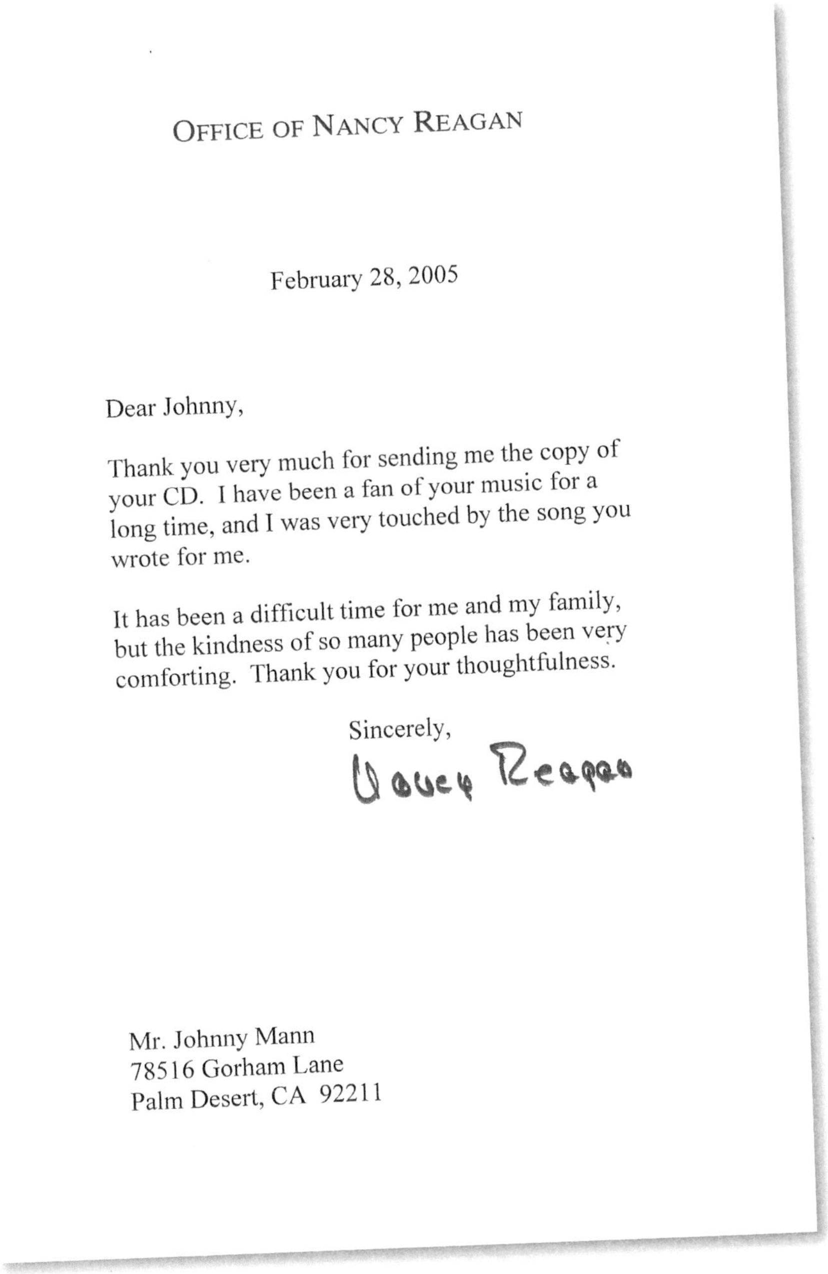

OFFICE OF NANCY REAGAN

February 28, 2005

Dear Johnny,

Thank you very much for sending me the copy of your CD. I have been a fan of your music for a long time, and I was very touched by the song you wrote for me.

It has been a difficult time for me and my family, but the kindness of so many people has been very comforting. Thank you for your thoughtfulness.

Sincerely,

Nancy Reagan

Mr. Johnny Mann
78516 Gorham Lane
Palm Desert, CA 92211

Nancy Reagan's letter of thanks for the song I wrote for her

Betty and me with John Glenn, Betty and President Gerald Ford at the desert home of Bob and Delores Hope prior to the Gala Dinner benefiting Eisenhower Medical Center

I met George H.W. Bush at the home of Bob Hope while Bush was vice president. When I was introduced to him, I was astonished when he said very enthusiastically, "Oh, John, Cy talks about you all the time!" I was flabbergasted that he would associate me with Cy Laughter and his Bogie Busters Celebrity Golf Tournaments! I missed out on an opportunity to play in a foursome with President Ford in the desert once because I had a recording session I could not cancel. I would have loved to play golf with him and gotten to know him better. We did have a wonderful picture taken with him and his Betty, me and my Betty and Sen. John Glenn at the home of Bob Hope.

As I have grown older, my feelings for my country have gotten more intense. When people insult America, I react by expressing my patriotic feelings through music. You've read the words to "Voice of Freedom" and "Stand Up and Cheer" in earlier chapters. I wrote two more such songs fairly recently. One is "Only Through Her Eyes," which imagines what the

CONGRESS OF THE UNITED STATES
HOUSE OF REPRESENTATIVES
2411 *Rayburn Bldg.*
WASHINGTON, D. C. 20515

DAN BURTON , M.C.
6TH DISTRICT, INDIANA

March 3, 1997

Mr. Johnny Mann
78516 Gorham Lane
Palm Desert, California 92211

Dear Johnny:

Thanks for your very kind letter of February 18.

I sure miss your smiling face, and I hope the time comes
in the not too distant future when we can once again play
a little golf together.

Thank you very much for the prayers you're giving for me
and my colleagues during your daily devotions. We all certainly
need it, and I certainly appreciate it.

Please give my best wishes to your lovely wife, Betty, and
when you talk to Alvy and Carolyn Moore, I hope you'll give
them my best regards,

Thanks again for thinking of me, Johnny, and praying for
me.

Best regards,

Dan Burton
Member of Congress

DB:lrt

Statue of Liberty has seen as she holds her torch above New York harbor. The other is "One Nation Under God," which was a response to an effort in 2006 to take the words "under God" out of the Pledge of Allegiance.

I have recorded these songs with pro singers and included them on a CD I released with some of my older patriotic recordings. I know they will never be famous songs because patriotism isn't very popular any more, but I am proud of them, love to hear them sung, and hope you will find the words inspiring.

Only Through Her Eyes

NARRATION: The Statue of Liberty has stood at the gateway to America for more than one hundred years. She has become a symbol to the world of God's blessing upon this great land, for she has seen us grow into a nation that represents freedom to all who would pass beneath her flame. As future generations come and go, only she will be there to see the fulfillment of our dreams, a strong and glorious nation, striving to bring the message of God's love and peace to the entire world.

Only through her eyes can we see the longing;
Only through her eyes can we see the pain.
Only by her light can we see the people born of many nations
Only through her eyes.
Only from her eyes can they feel the welcome;
Only in her world can the dream come true.
Only in this land will they find the blessings of a home
and freedom
Only in this land.
If she could feel what made us seek the heights
And have the will to carry on.
If she but knew what made us fight the fights
Until all thought of fear was gone.
Then she would know what she has meant to a young land,
To a people who can say as one,
When we sleep at night we know the dawn will break on freedom.
For she has seen a nation grow from age to age,
She has seen the people come from lands afar.
She has heard our freedom ring from shore to shore.
America, we see these dreams fulfilled,
Only through her eyes.

Words and music by Johnny Mann, ASCAP, 2008

HOUSE OF REPRESENTATIVES
WASHINGTON, D. C. 20515

BARRY M. GOLDWATER, JR.
20TH DISTRICT
CALIFORNIA

July 4, 1982

Dear Johnny:

In your life, you've seen many things, you've been to many places, and you've sung many songs. But for you, Johnny, there's nothing better than singing America's song of freedom, in the greatest country on earth.

The Great American Choral Festival is a chance for you to share with others your love for America, through your talent in music. Your genuine spirit of patriotism is seen by all the Festival's participants, who could easily envision you in the role of "Uncle Sam" or "Yankee Doodle Dandy."

Maybe you weren't born on the Fourth of July, but you're clearly a true American, in heart, spirit, and song.

Best regards,

BARRY M. GOLDWATER, JR.
Member of Congress

Johnny Mann
Great American

THE WHITE HOUSE

WASHINGTON

June 23, 2008

Mr. John R. Mann
117 James Lawrence Orr Drive
Anderson, South Carolina 29621

Dear John:

The copy of your CD, *One Nation Under God*, made it to me in the
Oval Office. Thank you for thinking of Laura and me. Your patriotism
reflects the best of the American spirit.

Best wishes, and may God bless you.

Sincerely,

George W. Bush

George W. Bush's note about the *One Nation Under God* CD

One Nation Under God

We are a people who have a faith in God,
We are a nation of the free.
To live in God's glory, to dwell in his peace,
His blessings for all the world to see.
We wake with the dawn, a new day is here,
Our place is foreseen under God;
Our future is clear we follow a path
That leads through the land of the free.
Living our lives together
We share the joys that we have, the things we remember
We can believe when we end each day;
There will always be a free tomorrow.
Now is the time, a time for us all
To rise with our hopes and our prayers.
We have blessings to share, we have peace in our land;
One nation under God.

Words and music by Johnny Mann, ASCAP, 2008

Chapter Sixteen

AWAY DOWN SOUTH

Where on earth is Anderson, South Carolina?" That was the question Betty's daughter Stephanie Barr asked when her husband Jim was offered a job there in 2004. He accepted it, they moved down from Chicago, and we came out to visit them a few months later.

Anderson is in the northwest corner of South Carolina, in the foothills of the Blue Ridge Mountains and is located on a large, beautiful lake. Even though we visited in fall and winter, everything was green. Seeing trees and grass was a nice contrast to the desert landscape. We enjoyed the restaurants and so many things about this little city. I said to Betty one day, "Man, I could live here!" We decided just like that to do it. After eleven years, the social scene in Palm Desert had gotten old, and we had lost our dear friend Howard Keel to cancer a few months before. We were ready for a real retirement move. (Incidentally, even Judy Keel has moved to beautiful South Carolina to be near her daughter in Charleston!)

We really knew this was a God-directed move because everything fell into place so quickly. Our house in Palm Desert sold immediately to a couple from Canada, and by Mother's Day we had arrived in Anderson. We built a house in a conveniently located neighborhood and in no time at all, we had met a whole new community of music lovers.

Our Anderson family, Jim and Stephanie Barr

While we were still in the desert, Jim Barr called to say there was an ad in the Anderson newspaper looking for a music director for Anderson University. He said, "Do you want to go back to work?" Well, I made the call just to find out a little more and though I didn't pursue the job, that's how I met Byron Burns. Byron is an engineer at the local hospital system, AnMed Health, but he is also an excellent percussionist who plays in bands and orchestras all over the place, including the university.

It turned out the hospital was celebrating its hundredth anniversary and wanted to do a community concert like the ones I had led for Northridge Hospital. I wrote a song for their theme "We're In This Together" and met a lot of singers and musicians in the choir I conducted. Music people in Anderson, like music people everywhere, are very close-knit. It turns out that a lot of the people in the AnMed choir were also part of a community choir that presents a benefit concert each year for a local charity, the Cancer Association of Anderson. This Choir of Hope and Remembrance performed my arrangement of "You'll Never Walk Alone" one year, and some years later Betty and I joined the choir. This choir has performed a number of my musical arrangements and some of my original patriotic compositions, which has been so great.

By then we had become good friends with another couple who sing in the Choir of Hope, Doug and Jeanine Douglas, and its conductor Bob Heritage and his wife Carla. We eventually joined St. John's United Methodist Church, where Bob is the minister of music and the other three sing in the choir. Naturally, Betty and I joined that choir too and love all the activities at the church. We stay busy playing bridge, going out with friends – minus the tuxedo, most of the time – and I still do some jingle production. Betty points out that there is no mention of retirement in the Bible!

We also kept up our connections with Anderson University. Besides attending plays and musical events at this fine school – which has long-standing music and theatre departments – we were connected by Betty's sister Mary, who moved to Anderson from Chicago and took a job there. As Anderson University's hundredth anniversary approached,

With conductor and friend Dr. Robert Heritage at the Cancer Association of Anderson's Concert of Hope and Remembrance

I was asked to write a song to commemorate that. "The Sounds of Anderson" was adopted as the official alma mater for the new century.

And what do you know? In May 2010, Anderson University presented me with an honorary doctorate of humanities in recognition of my contributions to the world of music. It was my first honorary degree and I was thrilled. Not bad for a guy who only graduated from high school!

The Sounds of Anderson

The sounds of Anderson live in my heart.
Live in my memories, the sounds of joy;
The dreams of Anderson
Tell tales of tears and happiness in golden days gone by.
Seeds of learning will flourish;
New friends will guide us through the land.
These are the friendships we cherish
Touched by God's almighty hand
We know we love our alma mater;
We know the joy of life she brings,
Ah, but there's one thing only God can know:
What Anderson means to me.

Words and music by Johnny Mann, ASCAP, 2009

Chapter Seventeen

BRILLIANT IDEAS THAT WENT NOWHERE

Earlier in this book I told you about the gig I didn't get with Judy Garland, the marriage that never happened with Elizabeth Taylor and Kelsey Grammer's CD that was never released. Since I've promised to share my failures as well as my successes, this chapter is about a few more projects that went nowhere.

One of my greatest frustrations, which began in 1982, involves a beautiful piece of music I wrote for Mary Kay Cosmetics. This was the year I met Betty and she was selling Mary Kay at the time. I incorporated eight key phrases from the company's marketing and seminar brochure in the lyrics. The song "The Beauty of You" expresses founder Mary Kay Ash's philosophy of giving motivation, pride and opportunity to her sales women, while emphasizing respect for God, country and family. I recorded the song with eight male pro singers, a cappella. It's a gorgeous and lush piece of music that I thought was a perfect "alma mater" for Mary Kay Cosmetics.

I began my quest with an appointment at the company's Dallas headquarters with a top executive and didn't get very far because of the "It's not created here so we're not interested" syndrome. So I let it lie

April 17, 1995

Mr. Johnny Mann
78516 Gortham Lane
Bermuda Dunes, CA 92203

Dear Mr. Mann:

I received your letter and tape – and of course, I remember you! I have listened to your song and was delighted with it. I then shared it with our Director of Special Events, ███ ███████. He suggests that you contact him directly for further discussion to see if there is any way we could use your lyrics. He can be reached at (███) ████████.

Thank you so much for contacting me again. It was a pleasure hearing from you.

Sincerely,

Mary Kay

Mary Kay
Chairman Emeritus

MKA:jcm

cc: Ron Trammell

MARY KAY

Mary Kay Ash
Chairman Emeritus
Mary Kay Cosmetics, Inc.
8787 Stemmons Freeway
Dallas, Texas 75247

Letter from Mary Kay

for a decade. In 1995, I sent a CD directly to Mary Kay herself and she wrote me a lovely thank you note, reproduced here, but it still went nowhere. Since then, I've played the song for a number of Mary Kay saleswomen and directors from California, Illinois and South Carolina. Every one of them loved the song.

In 2013, I revisited the idea because of Mary Kay Cosmetics' upcoming fiftieth anniversary celebration. I played the song to two women executives at the Dallas headquarters and was told that they do not use any vocal music and prefer a pop, upbeat style rather than the beautiful ballad that I had written.

Bummer! I guess you can at least call me persistent, for working on this project for thirty years. The good news is I'm still married to Betty!

Another light bulb that went off in my head was the Jiffy Jotter. Before the Great American Choral Festival, I was always driving here and there and needed something handy for writing down notes. I developed a fold-up notebook containing a pad of paper and a pen. It could be attached to the middle of the front seat, then folded down and out of the way when not in use.

I worked with 3M, which had made a fortune on the Post-it note, to create a type of adhesive that attached the folder to the seat. A friend at General Motors gave me advice on the proper placement of the notebook. By the time I was really getting somewhere, General Motors changed the design of all its cars from a bench seat to two bucket seats with a gear shift unit in the middle and the Jiffy Jotter wouldn't work. Another bummer!

St. Patrick's Day Performance in Anderson with Cruz Control Quartet, Anderson Mayor Terence Roberts and me singing "My Wild Irish Rose" at 8:00am. Left to right, John Yane, me, Doug Douglas, Mayor Roberts, Norman Blankenship, and Richard Brennan

My last idea was truly brilliant and is making tons of money today, but unfortunately it's not making any money for me because I am not affiliated directly with a greeting card company. Many years ago, I recorded my own "Happy Birthday" musical message with the Johnny Mann Singers. I thought it would be great to have a birthday card you opened and the song would play. I contacted Hallmark Greetings but they wouldn't even let me send my idea to them because they said they don't use ideas from outside the company. Sound familiar?

Because I never sent my idea to Hallmark, I couldn't claim any creative ownership. However, just a few years later, I noticed many of the greeting card companies had put musical messages in their cards. Now you see them everywhere.

I've re-voiced the song so that a popular barbershop quartet here in Anderson can sing it. CruzControl -- Richard Brennan, tenor; Norman Blankenship, lead; John Yane, baritone; and Doug Douglas, bass -- sing it at their performances for people in the audience. I'm happy it is being enjoyed by many people who are celebrating birthdays and anniversaries, even if I don't make a dime on it.

If I get any more brain storms and they develop into something, you can be sure I'll be shouting it from the roof tops. Meanwhile, here are the lyrics of the Mary Kay Cosmetics song. I haven't given up!

The Beauty of You

The beauty of you will light up your life
Will flower within your heart as does the rose.
The beauty of you will show in your eyes
A vision of loveliness born of a dream.

Dreams may blossom or perish
Fragile like writings in the sand.
Life is the real dream we cherish
Touched by God's almighty hand.

The beauty of you will light up your life
And when you feel that glow
You'll want the world to know
The beauty of you, the beauty of Mary Kay
The beauty of Mary Kay.

Words and music by Johnny Mann, ASCAP, 1982

Chapter Eighteen

HOW SMALL WE ARE

Here is the way I can look at my life. I started with zero with parents who didn't have anything, then I got into music and it exploded. I went all the way to the top with my own national television series. When that was off the air, I met the love of my life, we lost everything and went all the way to the bottom. After that we started rebuilding, and we got to where we are now, debt-free, comfortable and home in Anderson – and we did it together with the Lord beside us every step of the way. I have had a wonderful life full of blessings, and it's not over yet!

In coming to the end of my story, I wondered what would best describe not only my feelings, but yours as well, I hope. The lyrics of this song by Earl Wilson, Jr. have stayed with me over many years, ever since I recorded it for one of my albums. I feel these words best express my innermost sentiments.

How Small We Are, How Little We Know

We laugh, we cry, we live, we die,
And when we're gone the world goes on.
We love, we hate, we learn too late

How small we are, how little we know.

We hear, we touch, we talk too much
Of things we have no knowledge of.
We see, we feel, yet can't conceal
How small we are, how little we know.

See how the time moves swiftly by,
We don't know how, we don't know why.
We reach so high and fall so low
The more we learn, the less we know.

Too soon the time to go will come,
Too late the will to carry on.
And so we leave too much undone.
How small we are, how little we know.

By permission, Earl Wilson, Jr., composer, lyricist

Chapter Nineteen

AFTERWORD: DEAR HEARTS AND GENTLE PEOPLE

Over my lifetime, I've been blessed to know a whole lot of people who have had a great influence on me and who have brought great joy to my life.

The first real friend I had as a child was **Bill Armentrout**, who lived next door to me in Baltimore. I talked about him in my first chapter – the boy who blew smoke rings for his mother's bridge-playing friends. We were the same age. His father was a pharmacist in the neighborhood and therefore his family was much better off than mine. Those smoke rings he blew eventually caused his demise from emphysema. He was discharged from the army because of his lung condition and lived on his army disability pension for the rest of his life. I gave him odd jobs during *Stand Up and Cheer* concert tours and Great American Choral Festival competitions. We had fun as youngsters and I loved him like a brother.

In life, you are lucky to have a true friend who is always there when you are down. I have been blessed to have that friend in **Roy Hollingsworth and his wife Diane.** At the worst time, Roy's strength and generosity helped me to get back on my feet. We've known each other sixty years and have shared personal and family experiences. When Betty and I had to stay somewhere to wait for our Palm Desert home to be completed, Roy offered his Palm Springs condo. I expected to pay the monthly rental fee, but he said, "Just pay the utilities." He made it easy! We have fond memories of the time we stayed there.

Many comedians in show business have the reputation for bad language and foul jokes. My old pal **Woody Woodbury** is a piano player and humorist. He tells stories in night clubs and country clubs and can keep listeners enthralled with his clean humor and audience involvement. A former World War II navy fighter pilot, he has had years of entertaining in television and movies. I so admire Woody. He's a real American. We keep in touch as much as distance allows.

Peggy Clark Schwartz, **Sue Allen Brown** and **Loulie Jean Norman** were my first female professional singers from The *NBC Comedy Hour*. Sue and Peg sang on hundreds of recordings over the years and Loulie sang on the albums and was the featured soprano voice on the song "Summertime" from the motion picture *Porgy and Bess*. I appreciated so much their friendship and putting up with me because of my being the young, new kid on the block. The relationship has lasted with Peg and Sue and their families since 1954! Loulie is now singing in the heavenly chorus.

Thurl Ravenscroft, the aforementioned voice of Tony the Tiger and known to me affectionately as Pappy, was irreplaceable as a dear friend who was always there for me. Obviously, when I needed that wonderful bass sound, low and strong or mellow, he was ready and willing. Along with a lifetime of singing, he had a successful career of voice-over recording for many commercials and for attractions at Disneyland and Walt Disney World. I miss him dearly.

Bill Cole was one of the singers who was instrumental later in my Christian walk. He was a wonderful studio singer and I used his tenor voice on all of my albums from the time he originally moved to Hollywood from Chicago. He introduced me to Ralph Carmichael and produced the recording of two Christian albums for the Johnny Mann Singers. We shared personal family time over the years and even co-owned a condo in Indian Wells, California. I owe it to Bill for having brought me closer to the Lord.

Clark Gassman and his wife Jan were dear friends, both musically talented. Clark and Bill Cole helped me learn about the Lord during Bible studies. Clark was the most quiet and humble man, yet he oozed musical ability. He was an arranger, composer and keyboardist who had a plethora of equipment in his home that enabled him to create complete orchestral sound far ahead of his time. I worked with him on projects and was always in awe of what he did. His only negative trait was the modesty about his own works. Since 2006, he's been busy creating original Heavenly music.

Clark on keyboard

John Caldwell was a businessman who I admired for his humble Christian life. He was an attorney I befriended and also used several times for legal advice. John was a typical lawyer in his dress – wing-tip shoes, Brooks Brothers suit and always a necktie – but atypical when compared to the average lawyer. Two stories come to mind about John. On one occasion in the desert, John and his wife Hester came over to relax at the pool, something he rarely did. While I was in the pool talking to someone else, John strolled out in his bathing trunks, a self-righteous grin on his face. He was also wearing a fashionable necktie! The other story is one John told about his Uncle Charlie, who had never seen an ocean except on TV. They were standing on the deck of John's modest San Clemente home overlooking the Pacific Ocean. John proudly motioned to the ocean and said, "What do you think?" Uncle Charlie hesitated and slowly replied, "Well...I thought it would be bigger." A sweet note about the Caldwells: They donated use of this home to many young missionary couples in training.

Another talented friend in Christian music is **Dan Burgess**. Dan and I have known each other for more than forty years. He has written hundreds of great songs and hymns. What a creative talent he is! We shared many musical experiences together and now he is helping me as producer of my latest radio jingle recording sessions in Nashville. I have personally chosen one of Dan's most popular songs, "Press On," to be played at my memorial service – many years from now, I hope!

During my years of involvement with Northridge Hospital, I developed a personal friendship with **Meredith Hale, M.D**. We became very close when he was head of rehabilitation and later director of the medical staff while I was serving on the hospital foundation board. We enjoyed our frequent match-ups at pool games at his home, doing our best to be the victor of the day. Meredith and his wife **Carol** made us honorary members of their wonderful family. We shared outings, meals and music, never tiring of each other. He served as a physician in two tours of duty in Vietnam combat zones. His stories are legendary. Another great American.

Dr. Meredith Hale was a worthy opponent and great friend

Today I feel so privileged to be part of what I call a brotherhood of musical professionals. My getting to know each one of these four musical directors came about in strange circumstances; one more way that the Lord blessed my life:

- I got a phone call one day from **Tom Hammett**, a church choir director in Chattanooga, Tennessee. He inquired about some of my arrangements to use in

Me, Betty, Tom and Faye Hammett

an upcoming concert. After much discussion, he asked if I would consider coming to the church to direct the choir myself. That was the beginning of what is now a personal family relationship. Tom's wife **Faye** and their four talented daughters make a true Christian musical family.

- Would you believe another phone call resulting in a request for Johnny Mann music came in early 2007 from **Terry Price**, director of music for Preston Hollow Presbyterian Church in Dallas, Texas. We hit it off immediately over the phone. Terry asked if I'd consider coming to Dallas and I said, "YES!" The occasion was his annual

Alyce and Terry Price from Dallas. Great hosts!

Americana Concert held in early June. Terry's wife **Alyce** and my Betty became as good friends as Terry and I did. We have maintained a close relationship with Terry and his choir. We've been back several times and have traveled together too.

- As I have said to **Jim Clancy** personally, he is the finest choral arranger and conductor bar none. He is also one of the nicest and most humble men in show business. I am privileged to have attended his Vocal Majority shows in Dallas with his group of over hundred-thirty male voices. Jim produces the most enjoyable sounds I have ever heard. We look forward to our Dallas visits to be able to see Jim and his wife **Judy** again.

- I came to live in Anderson, South Carolina in 2005 not having any idea of what I'd be involved in musically, if anything! As I mentioned, one of the music people I met after settling here is **Bob Heritage**. It is a pleasure for me to sing under Bob's direction both in the Concert of Hope and Remembrance and at St. John's United Methodist Church because he has a way of putting joy into the body of his choir. He is a wonderful conductor and a highly educated man, having earned his Ph.D. in music education. Consequently, his musical production is splendid!

Grown-up daughters, left to right: Jennifer, grandson Austin and mother Susie.

We enjoy the friendship of Bob and his wife **Carla,** our talented top soprano who can really pop out those high Cs.

A few more special musical people in my life who deserve mention and thanks include **Frank Granofsky** for his recommendation of me to the United States Army Field Band -- much more fun than Korea would have been – and **Richard Schulenburg**, for his creativity, help with my music reproduction and more importantly, being a real brother to me.

Since our move to Anderson, I am so grateful to **David L. Kyle, Jr.**, **MD**, for keeping me alive through his medical knowledge and constant care. He's the best medical quarterback I could hope to have. And, my love to my angel nurse **Nicole Whitfield** and all the other staff at Cornerstone Family Medicine.

And then there's my family. My daughters **Susie** and **Jennifer** and grandson **Austin**, I thank you for still loving me despite our living apart the majority of your years and mine. To step-kids **Stephanie, Jim** and **Pete:** I appreciate you for accepting me and for all the enjoyable times we've had together, especially during these Anderson years.

And, lastly, I thank my Savior **Jesus Christ** for the countless blessings, grace and mercy He extends to me daily.

ACKNOWLEDGMENTS

This book has been many years in the making, beginning with my friend David Van Gorder's interviews and tapes almost twenty years ago. Once we moved to Anderson, Kylie Yerka, an editor at the *Anderson Independent Mail*, Kylie Yerka, did a few more interviews. But we really got rolling in January 2013 when writer and editor Kathryn Smith, who we met through the Cancer Association of Anderson and its Concert of Hope, began coming to our home. She started with Kylie's notes and then recorded hours of conversations, helping me put these many memories into a cohesive book. In the process, she, Betty and I became great friends, enjoying not only conversation but cocktail hours when she came by in the afternoon.

From there, I want to thank Theresa O'Rourke, owner of PIP Printing and Marketing, and her talented designer Caryn Scheving, who came up with the book design and printed it so beautifully. The cartoon on the cover is the work of our late great friend, Buzz Gambill. Our good friends Jeanine and Doug Douglas used their computer and DVD creativity to take pictures, scan and edit them, and helped us select the best ones to include in the book. Betty's daughter Stephanie Barr was my photo scanner and proofreader, and Stephanie's husband Jim Barr, my webmaster, used his tech savvy to get the book into cyberspace. Kathryn Smith's mother Dot Yandle, also an editor and writer, was another proofreader for this book. Thanks to all of you!

Thanks to Paul Brown for his audio advice on taping the book, and accolades to Damon Downs, the engineer at Draisen-Edwards Music, who helped me put this book on tape and keeps all my music cataloged. He's a gem...and located only minutes from my home

Very special thanks to my friend Evans Whitaker, president of Anderson University, his wife Diane and his staff for their generosity in providing my book launch at the university's fine arts center.

I said it in my dedication and I'll say it again: Betty made me write this book, and I couldn't have done it without her!

Appendix

Johnny Mann
Discography

1956	*Night*
1959	*Alma Mater*
1960	*Roar Along with Singing 20s*
1960	*Swing Along with Singing 30s*
1961	*Ballads of The King*
1961	*Great Band with Great Voices*
1962	*Ballads of The King Vol. 2*
1962	*Swing the Great Voices of Great Bands*
1962	*Golden Folk Song Hits*
1963	*Golden Folk Song Hits Vol. 2*
1964	*Golden Folk Song Hits Vol. 3*
1964	*Invisible Tears*
1964	*Greatest of the Johnny Mann Singers at the Bottom of the Fair*
1965	*If I Loved You*
1965	*Roses and Rainbows*
1966	*Beatle Ballad*
1966	*I'll Always Remember You*
1966	*Flowing Voices*

1966	*Daydream*
1966	*Countryside*
1966	*Perfect Blend*
1967	*A Man and a Woman*
1967	*This is My Country*
1967	*We Wish You a Merry Christmas*
1967	*We Can Fly/Up, Up and Away*
1967	*Don't Look Back*
1968	*Love Is Blue*
1968	*Midnight Special*
1968	*This Guy's In Love With You*
1969	*Goodnight, My Love*
1969	*Golden*
1973	*So Proudly We Hail*
1973	*Stand Up and Cheer*
1975	*The Church's One Foundation*
1975	*The Four Freedoms*
1975	*Outer Space Inner Space*
2005	*Sixties Mann*
2006	*Best of the Johnny Mann Singers*
2006	*Let the Games Begin*
2006	*Praising His Name in Quiet Time*

Guest Stars on
Stand Up and Cheer

Patti Page

John Forsythe

Jack Jones

Forrest Tucker

Bobby Goldsboro

Florence Henderson

Della Reese

Edie Adams

Trini Lopez

Jimmy Dean

Roy Rogers, Dale Evans
and Family

Pat Boone

Dusty Springfield

Joey Bishop

Buddy Hackett

Lloyd Bridges

The Lennon Sisters

Vincent Price

Bobby Vinton

Mac Davis

Lou Rawls

Al Martino

JoAnne Worley

Joan Rivers

Mickey Rooney

James Darren

Peter Marshall

Rich Little

Jim Backus

Alex Karras

Jerry Lucas

Rod Serling

Bobbie Gentry

Joel Grey

Robert Morse

Phil Silvers

Ed Ames

Roger Miller

Cliff Robertson

John Davidson

Frank Gorshin

Bob Crane

Louis Nye

Mel Tormé

Don Knotts

Henry Mancini

Steve Allen

Dick Clark

The Everly Brothers

Arte Johnson

Milton Berle

Andy Griffith

Carol Lawrence

Totie Fields

Paul Williams

Hugh O'Brien

Marilyn Michaels

Wayne Newton

Don Rickles

The Lettermen

Lloyd Haynes

Lassie

Ken Berry

Corbett Monica

William Shatner

Eddy Arnold